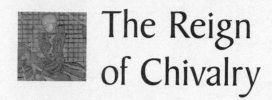

The Reign of Chivalry

The Reign
of Chivalry

Richard Barber

THE BOYDELL PRESS

First published 1980
David & Charles, Newton Abbot

New Edition 2005
The Boydell Press, Woodbridge

ISBN 1 84383 182 1

The Boydell Press is an imprint of Boydell & Brewer Ltd
PO Box 9, Woodbridge, Suffolk IP12 3DF, UK
and of Boydell & Brewer Inc.
668 Mt Hope Avenue, Rochester, NY 14620, USA

Designed by Tina Ranft

Contents

 # List of Illustrations

The Knight
and Warfare

I n every Western European language except English the word for knight
also means horseman: *chevalier, Ritter, cavaliere, caballero.* The English word
has quite another derivation, coming from the Anglo-Saxon *cniht,* a
servant; it is the same word as *Knecht* in modern German. The knight as a man
on horseback is a familiar image, but the knight as servant does not fit with our
preconceived ideas. Yet it is exactly this dual element, of skill in both
horsemanship and service, that gives the knight – and chivalry – its peculiar
quality.

Many accounts of chivalry begin with the hordes of barbarians such as the
Huns, who swept across the frontiers of the Roman Empire and who seemed
so inseparable from their horses that one classical writer called them 'shaggy
centaurs'. But to trace the origins of knighthood directly back to these
barbarians is just as much an error as that of the seventeenth-century historians
who firmly believed that orders of knighthood could be traced back to the
Roman class called 'equites' ('horsemen'). The barbarian hordes belong to the
early history of cavalry, rather than the beginnings of chivalry. The time and
place from which medieval knighthood emerged is very different: not the
declining years of the Roman Empire, but the declining years of its successor,
the empire of Charlemagne. Carolingian armies were primarily mounted
infantry: Charlemagne's predecessor, Charles Martel, had won his great victory
at Poitiers in 733 with dismounted troops who stood 'as motionless as a wall,
and frozen together like a block of ice' against the attacks of the Arab horsemen
who had overrun southern France. His soldiers were free men, and were
summoned to serve only because all free men owed a general duty of service.

The gathering at the 'field of May' each year, which marked the beginning of the campaigning season, was, therefore, primarily one of free men who would fight as footsoldiers in a pitched battle.

But in Charlemagne's day there were signs of change. Because military equipment was expensive – in particular because the freemen had to have horses even though they were footsoldiers – the practice grew of delegating the duty of service: four men might equip a fifth to serve on their behalf, and instead of a general levy, the army came to consist of semi-professional soldiers, supported by a sort of war tax, levied in kind, on all freemen. A set of fines were laid down for failure to do service, but in an economy where money was little used these were ineffective. It was simpler to pay the fighting man direct, out of the royal resources, and this began to happen in the century after Charlemagne's death. There was a simple and well-tried way of doing this, through the institution known as commendation, which had grown up during the centuries when central authority was weak and the menace of the barbarians ever-present. Commendation originally referred to an ordinary freeman, lacking a stronghold and reserves of his own, who 'commended' himself to a lord; the lord, in return for certain kinds of service – in labour or goods – would protect him and provide for him. The system had been extended to all royal servants, so that Charlemagne's 'comrades' or counts were bound to him by such a tie, and became his vassals, just like the emperor's most humble palace servant. The element of 'providing' in these contracts, originally dealt with by including the vassal in the lord's household, was now dealt with by giving him a grant of land. So when the emperors after Charlemagne needed reliable warriors to serve them, they adapted the system of vassalage to include military as well as non-military service. The mounted warrior in particular, whose equipment was very expensive, benefited from this new arrangement. In return for often quite extensive lands, he had to serve the king or the king's lieutenant, one of the great lords, in his wars for a specified period.

Such, in essence, was the history of the development of military service in the obscure times of the ninth and tenth centuries. But we still have not reached the medieval knight, at once 'horseman' and 'servant', by explaining the element of service. How did the change to cavalry, or rather to a new kind of cavalry, take place? The barbarian horsemen had been expert with missiles while on horseback, using bows and javelins: they would approach, fire a volley at the infantry and wheel away again until the resistance of the latter was broken. The Goths used heavy lances, and the Romans themselves developed heavily-armed cavalry, capable of charging down an enemy. But the critical elements, which transformed the role of the mounted warrior, were the development of the stirrup and the shoeing of horses.

The stirrup, an Eastern invention first recorded in China in the late fifth century, was known in Western Europe by the eighth century, but as far as we can tell from archaeology and the occasional pictures in manuscripts was not widely used until the ninth century. With stirrups, the horseman was much surer in the saddle: he could deliver a very powerful blow with a lance which had the full weight of man and horse behind it, and it was much more difficult for his opponent to unseat him. The cavalry charge against a wall of infantry became possible, and infantry were reduced to the role of supporting troops. Horses that were shod had a surer footing and could be ridden much further and over difficult terrain without breaking down.

Other innovations, difficult to date precisely, were produced in the troubled times of the ninth and tenth centuries: high saddles with raised ends, long pointed shields which covered the exposed side of a horseman, improved mail and armour and – another Eastern invention – the crossbow, worked by a mechanical winder and trigger to deliver a bolt which, under favourable circumstances, could pierce armour.

The exact nature of Charlemagne's army is still unclear, but it seems that his crack troops were indeed a small group of heavily-armed cavalry. The group was small simply because equipment was immensely expensive: an edict issued in 805 specified that mail-shirts or *byrnys* were only required of landowners holding over 300 acres, and although this was the most costly single item, it represented only one-quarter of the total outlay for a horseman whose full equipment was as follows: horse; lance, shield, sword and scabbard; helmet, leggings and mail-shirt. Because of the expense of the mail-shirt, many who owned horses and arms went without it and served as light cavalry, making up the bulk of the army. We know little about Charlemagne's tactics, but his campaigns were fought largely against the fierce, ill-disciplined pagans of Germany, in difficult country which was either heavily wooded or mountainous. The cavalry charge would have been of little use here. We get a glimpse of the horseman's skills at this period in Nithard's account of the games at Strasbourg in 842, after Charlemagne's warring grandsons had made peace.

They also often gathered to hold games, in the following manner. Everyone assembled in a place suited to this kind of spectacle, and the crowd stood on either side. First of all the Saxons, Gascons, Bretons and men of Austrasia charged in equal numbers, as if they were going to attack each other; then some of them turned, and covering themselves with their shields, pretended to try to flee from their comrades, who rode after them; then, changing their roles, they began to pursue those from whom they had at first fled; and finally the two kings, on horseback with all their young men, charged into the fugitives urging their men on with great shouts and brandishing their lances. And it was a sight worth seeing, partly because so many nobles took part, and partly because it was all done in such good order.

Thirteenth century embossed leather shield of Konrad I of Thuringia

The cavalry charge proper does not appear until horsemen are matched against horsemen; this occurs during the civil wars that followed the break-up of Charlemagne's empire, and after the general adoption of the stirrup. Moreover, the cavalry charge requires flat, open spaces, and it is not unreasonable to attribute the appearance of this new type of battle to France and the Low Countries in the ninth or tenth centuries. To counter the effects of the impact of a cavalry charge, armour became heavier and more elaborate, and the horseman turns into the specialist mounted warrior, the knight.

The fully-fledged knight, when he first appears in history around the year 1000, is a well-equipped horseman, a rich man compared with his fellows, who does military service in return for a land-holding – his fief or fee. His political roots lie in the late Carolingian Empire, his technical equipment and skills in new inventions made under Charlemagne and his successors. But for his attitudes and culture we must go back to the barbarian invaders. The Roman armies, certainly in the later days of the Empire, had no great *esprit de corps*, particularly since they consisted of a vast potpourri of different races. The barbarian invaders lived and fought in small close-knit tribal groups, in which the warriors were not hirelings of the state, but were themselves the ruling élite, the comrades of the chieftain who led them. Although the knight was technically once more a hired servant, he retained the old ideals of the Germanic races, loyal to fellow-warriors and to the lord. This loyalty reinforced the purely practical bonds of vassalage, and at best became a devotion as remarkable as that of the Saxon Byrhtwold who refused to leave Byrhtnoth, his leader, after the defeat of the Saxons at Maldon in 991:

> Byrhtwold grasped his shield and spoke.
> He was an old companion. He brandished his ash-spear
> And with wonderful courage exhorted the warriors:
> 'Mind must be the firmer, heart the more fierce,
> Courage the greater, as our strength diminishes.
> Here lies our leader, dead, an heroic man in the dust.
> He who now longs to escape will lament for ever.
> I am old. I will not go from here,
> But I mean to lie by the side of my lord,
> Lie in the dust with the man I loved so dearly.'

The Saxons who fought beside Byrhtwold, the mounted warriors of Charlemagne's armies, the Viking invaders who won Normandy, were all to some extent a *corps d'élite*, men who lived for fighting. But their weapons and skills were relatively limited, and the knight's status was proportionally greater than that of his forerunners because his training was exceptional. He was not without rivals, however: the first mercenary soldiers appear in the eleventh century, ferocious and effective, serving for pay rather than the long-term benefits of the fief. But they were rootless, without a place in society, ready to betray their masters if the money ran out. A king who relied too much on mercenaries risked not only treachery but also was liable to alienate his barons, as King John did by using men like Fawkes de Breauté. Mercenary bands were also primarily mounted infantry, usually from Flanders; they consisted largely of supporting troops with only a handful of fully-armed men.

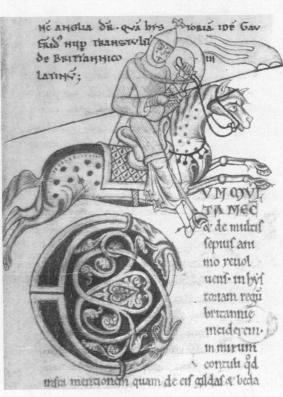

(above) *A Norman knight, from a manuscript of Geoffrey of Monmouth's* History of the Kings of Britain

(opposite) *Mounted man-at-arms on an armoured horse: the peak of the armourer's technique, with the arms inlaid into the breastplate*

The king needed an army at irregular intervals, his money revenues were small, and his resources were largely land. Hence the knight was paid by a long-term contract, in the form of a grant of land from which he could provide for himself and earn enough revenue to equip himself, and in return for which he served the king for a specified period each year. This shaped the knight's character and status. The Normans, descendants of the freebooting, roving Vikings, became settled landowners when they became knights. Because land was involved, knighthood became an hereditary caste and the title and obligations of knighthood passed with the land from the knight to his heir. But the social and economic implications of medieval knighthood lie outside our scope: we are concerned with the man on horseback, not knights in their other guise as lords or royal servants.

A knight had to learn a wide variety of skills, both in horsemanship and in the art of using weapons. Such training was usually given by placing the would-be knight in a large household, where there would be a number of squires (*écuyers*, bearers of the *écu* or shield) serving their apprenticeship in arms. This system persisted throughout the medieval period, but the next step,

the gaining of practical experience, changed considerably over the centuries. In the tenth and eleventh centuries, the squire would probably have his first taste of warfare in some private quarrel – a matter of skirmishes, ambushes and petty brawls. With the gradual suppression of private war everywhere except in Germany, the scene of the squire's initiation became large-scale campaigns, such as the Anglo-French campaigns of the twelfth century, or the crusades. In the fourteenth century he might also take part in the freebooting raids of the so-called 'free companies' in France, and similarly the Wars of the Roses in England offered opportunities in what was virtually a return to private war. In whatever kind of war he first fought, he acted both as an assistant to the knight, looking after his equipment and horses, and as a kind of light cavalry, less heavily armed than his master and so better equipped for raiding or pursuit.

Unless he came from a high-ranking family, the squire might have to wait many years before he could either afford to become a knight or could 'win his spurs' by some notable action. Suitable candidates were often knighted before a battle, though on two occasions Froissart records that soldiers shouting at a hare which had found its way between the lines drawn up in readiness for battle led to a hasty knighting of squires, because the shouts were mistaken for the beginning of the battle. Even when the squire had been knighted, he had not overcome all his problems, because he now had to 'maintain his estate'. To this end, knighting in the heat of battle was usually followed, sooner or later, by a grant of money or lands: thus Edward III, having knighted Neil Loring for his distinguished service at the battle of Sluys on 24 June 1340, granted him an annuity of £20 per annum on 26 June. Against this, we have records from southern France showing that some men who were of knightly rank were too poor to take up knighthood, even though they retained the title of squire (*bacheler*) to the end of their lives. This was usually due to a change in the family's fortunes: in southern France, where the laws of primogeniture did not apply, estates were divided equally among the heirs, and often reduced to minute portions. On the other hand, in northern France, Germany and England, the bulk of the estates went to the first-born male, leaving the younger sons to make their way in the world as best they could.

It is among these younger sons that the cult of chivalry, as opposed to knighthood pure and simple, began to develop in the late twelfth century. Such men, if they chose to try to make a living by the sword, might often spend twenty years fighting almost as mercenaries, dependent on their lord's generosity, before they won lands of their own or married an heiress. Without

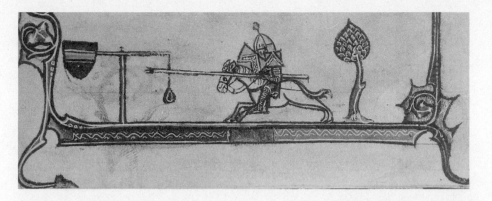

the cares and responsibilities of estates, living only for warfare, their unreal existence gave ample time for leisure, for listening to minstrels and practising the mock warfare known as tournaments. Tournaments were central to the world of chivalry: they acted both as training grounds for knights, now that private wars had almost disappeared, and as focal points for a literature and culture based on knighthood.

Let us look in detail at the career of one of the most famous warriors of the age, William Marshal, who began as a landless younger son, and ended as Regent of England and Earl of Pembroke. After his death, one of his household minstrels wrote a long poem about his career, which draws on William's own

(above) *Mounted knight tilting at the quintain, a form of training which taught lance-handling and steady riding*

(below) *Effigy of William Marshal, who rose from being a simple squire to earl marshal of England, in part through his skill in tournament*

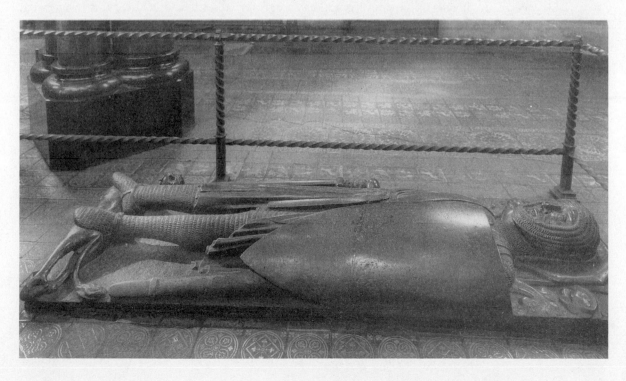

memories to give a vivid picture of a knight's life in tournaments and war in the late twelfth century.

William was born about 1144, the son of John FitzGilbert, marshal to Henry I of England. His father supported the Empress Matilda in the civil wars, and in 1152 he and his family were besieged at Newbury in Wiltshire by King Stephen. William's father arranged a truce, giving William as one of the hostages and promising that he would surrender the castle at the end of the truce. On the day appointed, however, he refused to honour the terms, having refortified the castle in the interval. Stephen's men were in favour of putting William into a siege-engine and hurling him at the castle, but when FitzGilbert was told of his son's intended fate he merely said: 'Do you what you like; I still have the hammers and anvil on which to forge a better one than him.' Despite FitzGilbert's obstinacy, the King was so taken by the child that he refused to allow him to be harmed. When peace was made in 1153, William was reunited with his family.

In about 1155 William was sent to the Count of Tancarville to be trained as a squire. One of the best descriptions of what this training in arms and general education involved is to be found in Chrétien de Troyes' *Perceval*, written for Philip of Flanders at almost exactly the time when William Marshal was at the height of his career as a tourneyer. Perceval's father was killed in battle against the heathens before the birth of his son; Perceval is therefore brought up by his mother far from knightly society, lest he should suffer the same fate. But a chance encounter with five knights arouses his curiosity, and he sets out into the world. His adventures, which include the killing of a knight with his javelin, bring him to the castle belonging to Gornemanz who, realising the true worth of this uncouth figure, clad in deerskin and the dead knight's armour, offers to instruct him. First the deerskins are removed and he is properly dressed and armed. Then spurs are brought, he mounts his horse, and Gornemanz hangs a shield round his neck, gives him a lance and says; 'Now, my friend, learn about weapons, and take heed how to hold a lance, and how to spur on and rein in a horse.' He makes him lean forward on the horse's neck and puts the lance in the rest on the saddle, and passes on to Perceval all that he knows about shield, sword and lance, because Gornemanz had been taught such things from his earliest childhood. Perceval, as one would expect of the hero in a romance, learns all this at once, and immediately handles his mount and weapons expertly, as if he had been doing it all his life; in reality, a knight's skills needed many hours of practice to bring them to an acceptable standard.

Gornemanz then instructs him in the sequence of the fight: first the knights engaged with lances until those were shattered, and only then drew their swords. The next day he formally knights Perceval, putting on his right spur and girding on his sword. When Perceval takes his leave he is transformed from a rustic in knight's armour into a fully-fledged member of the order of knighthood.

William Marshal's training was rather longer: he spent some eight years in the Count of Tancarville's household, 'doing nothing but drinking, eating and sleeping', until his companions teased him for it; the Count, however, is said to have recognised his talents. In 1168 he was in Poitou, in the service of his uncle Patrick, Earl of Salisbury, when the latter, escorting Queen Eleanor, was killed in an ambush laid by Geoffrey de Lusignan. He himself was wounded and taken prisoner but the Queen arranged for him to be ransomed and rewarded him for his courage with horses, armour, money and rich clothes. On his return to England, he was chosen by Henry II to act as a kind of 'tutor-in-arms' to his eldest son, Henry the young King, who was crowned in 1170. William took his charge abroad and they participated in tournaments, but disputes between father and son led to the civil war of 1173–4, in which William stayed with the young King. Indeed, he was one of his most trusted friends, and knighted the young King at some time in 1174, a great honour for a landless knight. Yet he seems to have retained the friendship of Henry II despite his master's rebellion.

The settlement of 1174, largely dictated by the older Henry, was followed by some years of peace, during which William and his protégé indulged their fondness for tournaments to the full. Their chief opponent was the young Count of Flanders, Philip, who had gathered some of the finest knights in Europe around him. At first the young King did badly, and was often defeated; the Normans and English had no great reputation as jousters. But in due course Henry's persistence and William's training were rewarded, and the French and Flemish had to acknowledge the young King as their equal. Indeed, if we are to believe William's biographer:

> It was the young King who revived chivalry which at this time was almost dead. He was the gateway through which she returned, and he was her standardbearer. For then great men did nothing for knights, but he set them an example by retaining good men. And the other lords, seeing such men gather round him, regarded him as very wise, because they knew that

no king or count is worth anything without good men at his side. They too started to do the same, retaining good knights and putting chivalry into good shape again. The Count of Flanders did likewise, envying the young King and wishing to demonstrate his own prowess. King, count and lords all sought out good knights and gave them horses and arms and money, land or good maintenance. But now the great men have put chivalry in prison again by their idleness, and their miserly ways have locked up generosity: tournaments have been abandoned in favour of lawsuits.

William's biographer describes two or three tournaments from this golden age of chivalry in detail. By this time William had become an experienced fighter, and he is very much the hero of the day: his earlier lack of success while he and Henry were gaining experience is passed over in a line or two – as one would expect – but, once he has the upper hand, his biographer describes it all in detail. Take, for example, a tournament at Lagny-sur-Marne: the young King had two hundred knights in his squadron, and there were nineteen counts and the Duke of Burgundy present, with a total of three thousand knights. Even allowing for the usual over-estimate of numbers by the chronicler, there must have been at least a thousand participants. The first attack was by men in the service of the lesser nobles; broken lances fell to the ground in such numbers that they almost prevented the horses from charging, and even before the young King and the Count of Flanders entered the field, the fighting was excellent.

The young King was next to charge into the fray, while the Count of Flanders held his men back; but Henry's men rode in with such impetus that he found himself alone in the rear while the opposition disappeared into the vineyard on the far side of the battleground. However, he saw a group of about forty knights to his right and rode off to attack them, breaking his lance on one of them. He was at once surrounded, and William and another knight, William des Préaux, rode up to rescue him. Des Préaux had already been taken prisoner that day, and had lost his armour: all he had on was a mailcoat and helmet. They seized Henry's horse and dragged him out of the mêlée, but the young King had to cover des Préaux with his shield, while William rained blows on his would-be captors. Even so, the young King's helmet was torn off before they made their escape.

The Count of Flanders now attacked Henry's weary knights, who were forced to retreat. Geoffrey, Count of Brittany, the young King's brother, tried to cover the retreat and unhorsed a number of knights, but was unable to fight off the Flemish alone; meanwhile a troop of thirty or so Flemish knights attacked the young King himself from another quarter, only to be beaten off by William, who was glad to make his escape with his master.

Defeat in a tournament could be expensive: des Préaux's loss of his armour

A lady arms her knight for a tournament, and welcomes him on his return

would have been a serious blow. But William was usually on the winning side: at a tournament at Eu, he took twelve horses in one day. He also formed a partnership with another knight of the young King's household, and spent two years travelling to tournaments with him. One of the young King's clerks recorded that between Whitsun and Lent they took prisoner one hundred and three knights, not counting horses and equipment, which were not written down in the records. The fact that the young King's clerks recorded these knights in their accounts separately from the other items implies that a captured knight often paid a ransom, perhaps as an alternative to losing horse and armour. Horses suitable for warfare and tournaments commanded enormous prices: a first-class warhorse cost ten to thirty times as much as an ordinary 'horse for the march'. A knight would probably need at least three such horses if he was to be properly equipped. William and his partner Roger de Gaugi not only made their reputation as warriors, but also won a small fortune; and certainly his biographer never refers again to the poverty which had hindered his first efforts as squire and knight.

Other episodes from William's career as tourneyer tell us more about the sport. We have already seen how there were no effective boundaries, and at a tournament west of Paris we find William attacking knights who had shut themselves up in an old wooden castle, having first tied their horses to the fence outside, or rescuing a group of knights shut up in a grange by their opponents. At an earlier tournament at the same place, he had taken a knight prisoner and was riding back to his lodging in the town leading his captive on horseback. On the way the knight used an overhanging drainpipe to swing off his horse, leaving William with only an empty horse when he arrived at his lodging. On another occasion some knights who came to present William with a prize found him at the blacksmith with his head on the anvil, having his helmet wrenched off; it was so battered he could not undo the fastenings.

The overall impression is of a cheerful companionship of knights, prepared to risk their lives in a sport which was little more than a violent free-for-all, but with a developing code of honour and behaviour. The 'rules' of tournaments at this period are difficult to decipher. In one episode William captures two horses but has them taken from him, yet he is able to recover them by complaining to the lords about the knights who have taken the horses. Likewise, the tactic used by the Count of Flanders of waiting until the rest of the tourneyers were in disarray and weary is treated with a mixture of admiration and disapproval, as though it were efficient but dishonourable!

One reason for the growing organisation of tournaments and the introduction of rules was that it was an exceptionally dangerous sport, although William's biographer does not depict its darker side. Even the supposed inventor of tournaments, Godfrey of Preuilly, was said to have been killed in one in 1066, and the roll-call of victims is substantial, down to the moment when Henri II of France was killed in a joust in 1559 because the Constable de Montgomeri had failed to drop the butt of a broken lance and the splintered end went through the King's visor. So early in the next century we find mock-warfare replacing the all too realistic fighting of William's tourneying days, with linen armour or blunted weapons instead of the full panoply of war.

William's career in tournaments spanned about twelve years, from 1171 to 1182. In the autumn of 1182, other knights of the young King's entourage, jealous of his standing with the young King, accused him of being the lover of the young King's wife Margaret (an echo, perhaps, of Lancelot's love for Guinevere at Arthur's court?). William denied the charges but the young King no longer treated him as a close friend, and Margaret went to her half-brother's court at Paris early the following year, by which time William had left for his estates in Normandy. When the accusations were finally disproved, and William rejoined the young King, civil war between son and father had been renewed; it ended with the young King's death from fever in June 1183. On his deathbed he charged William with the fulfilment of his vow to go on crusade, and William spent the next two years in Palestine, about which his biographer tells us nothing.

William returned to find the old tension between England and France renewed in the warfare which darkened Henry II's last days. He became a close friend and adviser of Henry and it was William, once branded traitor for supporting the young King in 1173–4, who was with the old King in his last desperate days. In the summer of 1189 Henry, defeated by the sudden alliance of Richard Coeur de Lion and Philip Augustus of France, was driven out of Le Mans and, seriously ill, went to Chinon on the Loire, where he died on 6 July. William had to make the arrangements for his funeral and burial at the abbey of Fontévrault and waited to meet Richard, whom he had unhorsed a few days earlier while covering Henry's retreat. Richard accused William of trying to kill him saying that he had only turned aside the lance by his strength of arm. But William replied that he was a good enough warrior to make sure that his lance found its mark, and if he had wanted to kill him he would have done so. Richard accepted his version, and not only pardoned him but sent him to

England as his representative to secure the kingdom for him. William's career – he was now forty-five – was now to be as much political as military. Having already been on crusade, he did not accompany Richard to Palestine, but was left as one of the council governing England. The warfare he experienced under Richard was small-scale, similar to the civil wars of Henry's reign – skirmishes, brief sieges and raids rather than full-scale battles. He showed himself to be a good tactician as well as a brave fighter. In an engagement near Vendôme, when Richard defeated and pursued Philip Augustus, William refused to join in the pursuit, but remained with a troop which he had reserved to cover a possible return of the French. In the event, the precaution was unnecessary, but Richard praised his action and declared that he had done better than all the other knights. On other occasions William was less restrained, and in an attack on the castle of Milli, Richard reproved him for leading the attack, saying that a man as important as he should not risk himself but should leave such exploits to younger men.

After Richard's death, William found himself out of favour at court for long periods, and it was only at the end of John's reign that he returned to both politics and warfare. During the campaigns in the months between the signing of Magna Carta in June 1215 and John's death in October 1216, he played a leading part in defending England against an invasion led by Prince Louis of France, and on the King's death was chosen as Henry III's guardian and Regent of England. He succeeded in trapping Louis at Winchelsea early in 1217; but he was unable to maintain the blockade, and Louis was able to make his escape, embarking at Dover.

Two months later Louis returned with a larger army and William, who had been reducing the castles held by Louis' allies one by one, was faced by a critical situation. The French divided their forces, and one part of the army went to attack Lincoln. William decided to challenge them, and with only 416 knights and 317 crossbowmen, he led the attack against a French force of 611 knights and about 1,000 footsoldiers entrenched in the town, and drove them out with considerable losses. Louis sent for reinforcements, but when these were defeated in a sea-battle, he sued for peace and withdrew to France. William had accomplished the task he had set himself, he was now over seventy and he asked to be relieved of his office early in 1219. He became a member of the Order of Knights Templar, and died later that year, 'full of years and honour'.

William Marshal's career is a remarkable one, but in its outlines it corresponds to the careers of many lesser knights whose fortunes were far from brilliant. The pattern of early training and tournaments leading to real warfare, and retirement from the battlefield to politics, is typical; the landless knights might spend longer at tournaments or in royal armies, but it was unusual to find any member of a noble family who did not spend much of his life up to the age of thirty under arms, unless he went into the Church; and in the early Middle Ages there are plenty of examples of churchmen whose knightly blood ran stronger than their ecclesiastical scruples. On the other hand, it is noticeable that William Marshal never took part in a major pitched battle before the battle at Lincoln, nor does he seem to have undertaken a major siege. Both these kinds of military action were relatively uncommon in the twelfth century, and we must move forward to the fourteenth century before we find knights with wide experience of both.

Twelfth-century warfare was relatively small-scale and informal, because the forces deployed were small, and discipline was poor. However, the beginnings of tactical thinking can be seen even in some of the skirmishes. Large engagements did take place in Palestine: it was here that Richard I fought his only pitched battles, against Saladin. Another exceptional occasion was the battle of Bouvines in 1214, probably fought on a larger scale than any other engagement during the twelfth or thirteenth centuries. Philip Augustus of France, with some 1,200 knights, faced a combined Flemish and German imperial army under Otto of some 1,500 knights, each side having about four times as man) footsoldiers. Philip knew that the imperial army was in the neighbourhood, and he and his advisers deliberately chose an area where cavalry charges would be effective – an open slope above the River Marcq near the village of Bouvines on the border between France and Flanders, clear of the surrounding marshes. The French drew up in reasonable order, across a Roman road, and were resting when the enemy vanguard made contact.

The allied army was on the march when the first of its troops went into the attack, and the main body had to be hurriedly put into battle order as they arrived; the whole column may have been as much as five miles long. By early afternoon the two armies were spread out in a thin line on a front just over a mile long. The French had had time to deploy their men carefully, selecting the best knights to form the front line, and had rested for an hour or two.

The first engagement was on the right wing, but although the Count of St Pol and his French knights charged right through the Flemish line, re-formed and attacked them from the rear, the fighting went on indecisively for three hours until the Count of Flanders himself was unhorsed, wounded and captured. In the centre, the Emperor Otto opened the attack, breaking up the French ranks; his pikemen pulled many knights off their horses, and Philip Augustus himself was unhorsed. However, the French re-formed and mounted a counter-attack; in the hand-to-hand fighting, Otto was unhorsed and, when the left wing of his army was defeated, his men were also overwhelmed. He himself was forced to flee, but on the right wing the Count of Dammartin and the Earl of Salisbury held out. Dammartin's tactic seem to have been unusual: he used a circle of pikemen, two deep, who formed a kind of fortress into which he and his knights could retire at the end of each charge. However, the Earl of Salisbury was captured after the Bishop of Beauvais had given him a tremendous blow with mace (bishops were not allowed to shed blood, and so used maces or clubs). Dammartin's men were reduced in number at each charge until only a handful were left, and when Dammartin's horse was wounded he himself was captured. Even so, the pikemen fought on and were only despatched after a long struggle.

Philip won his victory largely because his army was rested and in good order, and he allowed the enemy to make the first attack. Despite the shock value of a cavalry charge, again and again in medieval warfare a well-prepared defensive position decided the battle, particularly when it was between two forces of similar size and nature. A charge was exhausting, and repeated charges against an enemy who held steady could fail because the oncoming riders grew weary: if an army was to win the battle, it had to do so in the early stages. Again, the events at Bouvines confirm this, because Otto's first charge did almost succeed.

The actual nature of the fighting followed a set pattern: first a charge with lances, followed by a fierce mêlée of individual hand-to-hand struggles, in which swords, daggers and even wrestling were used – a French knight, Guillaume des Barres, seized the emperor from behind and tried to drag him from his horse but was unable to unseat him. To be unhorsed was very serious for a knight for even if he could find another horse in the confusion, it was difficult to remount in full armour. Philip Augustus was able to do so only because he was very fit. The part played by the footsoldiers in the battle was slight, apart from the Flemish pikemen. The French footsoldiers are hardly mentioned while the bulk of the imperial footsoldiers scarcely seem to have taken part in the fighting: many of them left the field without striking a blow. The pikemen, however, posed a more serious challenge to the knight with their long weapons they could lunge out and pull a knight down or wound his horse before they were within reach of the knight's sword. There were a few crossbowmen on the French side; none are mentioned on the imperial army, and their part in the battle seems to have been confined to the very first attack.

Bouvines is probably the best example of a 'chivalric' battle, in which the knights dominated and decided the course of the action. It is arguable that from the mid-thirteenth century onwards, developments in warfare were generally against the knight, and the ethos of his training was also becoming a handicap. Taking the latter point first, we have seen how tournaments in William Marshal's day placed considerable value on individual prowess, but were none the less exercises in fighting as a team, using battlefield, tactics and conditions. From the early thirteenth century onwards, there was an increasing emphasis on the individual, on the quest for the best knight, and single combat rather than mass fighting became the rule of the day, jousts rather than tournaments. The joust never replaced the tournament proper, but it did increase the emphasis placed on individual performances in the tournament. In William Marshal's day, we only once hear of a prize being given to the best knight, and that is a fine pike (the fish, not the weapon) presented informally by some of the lords. From the thirteenth century, the best knight in both jousts and in the tournament was usually singled out. We shall see the effect of this on the battlefield in due course, but first let us look at a thirteenth-century tournament.

In October 1285, a tournament was held at Chauvency, in north-east France, and a local poet, Jacques Bretex, has left a full account of it. It was announced some weeks beforehand, and knights came from a wide area to take part. The organisation was carried out by heralds, who not only spread word of the festivities, but acted as masters of ceremonies and commentators, identifying each contestant by his coat of arms and crying out his name. The company assembled on a Sunday, and Bretex was greeted by one of the heralds, who pointed out the most important knights to him at the dance held at the castle of Chauvency that evening.

On the Monday the jousting began in the morning, even though the dance had ended well after midnight. The knights heard Mass, then everyone went to the scene of the jousts outside the castle walls: the ladies seated themselves on the scaffolds erected for the occasion, while general confusion reigned below, until the first joust began. As the knights rode into the jousting area, or lists, their heralds called out their names. Bretex describes six jousts in the morning: perhaps it is poetic licence, but all the knights successfully break their lances, whereas later jousting records show that it was not uncommon for them to miss each other altogether. The injuries are fairly formidable: the first jouster breaks an arm when both horses fall, and at the fifth encounter knights and horses fall with such violence that both knights are feared to be dead. Between jousts the heralds address the ladies and point out how the knights are risking lives and limbs to win their favour. A new company of knights arrives at noon and the jousting continues in the afternoon until sunset. Then the ladies come down from the stands and the whole company returns to the castle; as they go, ladies and knights sing, and this musical contest continues during and after the great banquet in the castle that night, 'each one trying to carry off the prize'. There is dancing after the banquet and it is very late before the company retire.

On the Tuesday, the knights rise at dawn to prepare for the jousting Bretex records eight jousts, but as most of these are said to have taken place in the late afternoon, this is evidently only a small proportion of those actually fought. At the end of one joust a herald cries: 'Gérard of Looz burns with courage, prowess and boldness, and as soon as he has taken off his helmet steeps himself in courtesy, loyalty and generosity. He is like that both in the lists and at the castle.' This neat summary of knightly virtues so appeals to Bretex that he goes

*Misericord from Lincoln
Cathedral, showing a
knight falling during a
joust*

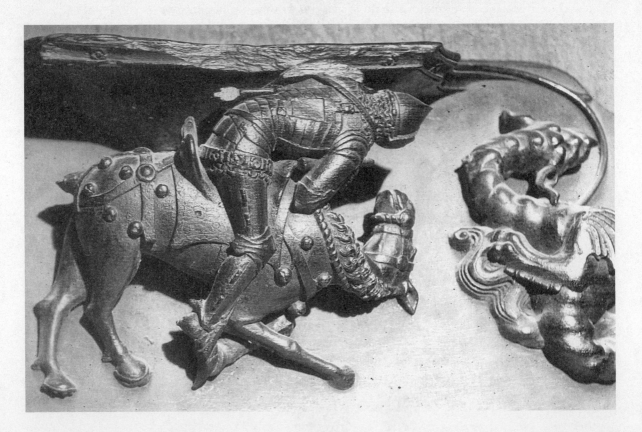

over to talk to the herald, and they become firm friends. When evening comes, there is once more a procession back to the castle, with songs on the way; after dinner there are plays and diversions as well as dancing and singing. A young girl dressed as a boy gracefully plays the clown. Before they go to bed, the knights decide to hold a general tourney on Thursday, and the heralds are sent out to invite all comers.

Wednesday is a rest day, and the teams for the two sides are chosen. Everyone agrees that a tourney is more exciting than jousts, and there is a general air of expectation: the knights boast of the feats they will perform the next day, and mock each other's claims. On Thursday the knights rise early and hear Mass, but they are slow to leave the castle because they are listening to the ladies singing: the heralds reproach them for their tardiness, at which everyone pours out of the castle at once. Horses neigh, there is a din of trumpets, drums, horns and bugles, while the sun glints on the armour and trappings of the great lords. The knights gather at the appointed place. By afternoon, after long delays, the opposing sides are ready, divided into four battles. No lances are used; the fighting is only with swords and clubs. The signal for the attack is given, and one knight distinguishes himself by hurling himself on the enemy before all the others; he fights so well that he holds off all his attackers until his friends come and join the mêlée. Helms and clubs are broken, lips and faces wounded, stirrups torn off, reins broken. Knights and horses alike sweat with exertion, tension and heat. The squires help their lords as best they can, while servants run in to gather up the pieces of weapons and armour, and the rich gloves and equipment, which they stuff into sacks. By the end of the afternoon the tourney has become four or five separate fights, each made up of duelling knights, scattered around the fields. Occasionally a group of knights come close to the stands; but much of the fighting has to be described to the ladies by the sharp-eyed heralds or by Bretex himself. At nightfall it is impossible to tell friend from foe, and the adversaries make their way home: those who have won rejoice in their good fortune, while the vanquished ride two to a broken-down old horse in order to get home. After dinner, when the dancing ends, the ladies and knights visit the wounded in their rooms, and entertain them with stories and games. Bretex himself sings of the great lovers of the past, and it is almost dawn before everyone is in bed.

After Mass the next morning, everyone departs for their homes, with great bustle and confusion. Lovers say fond farewells, and after a last song, the company disperses.

Although tournaments became more civilised during the thirteenth century, they were still a dangerous sport, as the wounded knights at Chauvency remind us. In particular, they could be used as a cover for settling old feuds: it was easy enough to pretend that a sharp weapon of war had been picked up by mistake instead of a blunted jousting sword. There was also the danger, in troubled times, that a tournament could be an excuse for gathering an army, and it was for this reason that they were banned in England for many years of Henry III's reign. Even in the best-regulated circles, opponents could lose their tempers, and the tournament could become a miniature war: this happened at Châlons in 1273, though much of the disorder was due to the bystanders. Edward I on his way back from crusade, challenged the Count of Châlons to a tournament, and in the mêlée, the two fought a prolonged duel, which ended by the Count trying to drag Edward from his horse – an accepted manoeuvre. Edward was tall enough and strong enough to lift the Count out of the saddle, and he galloped away with the Count still clinging to him. At this the Burgundian onlookers rioted and attacked the English, and the affair degenerated into a brawl.

Despite these risks, tournaments remained popular with great lords: for Edward III and the Black Prince were enthusiastic tourneyers, and great occasions were frequently marked by tournaments, which became more and more theatrical. We find the King, the Prince and their entourage appearing as the Pope and cardinals or the Lord Mayor and aldermen of London, and even proposing to ride into the lists dressed as the Seven Deadly Sins. The mere, project for this last tournament (which never actually took place) was, according to one chronicler, the reason for the appearance of a large number of evil spirits which were the air all that summer.

Edward and his son enjoyed tournaments, but they no longer regarded them as directly related to real warfare. They might teach individual knights how to handle their weapons and encourage warlike skills; but the tactics involved bore little relationship to what happened on a fourteenth-century battlefield, except perhaps in the last phases, when the combatants met hand to hand. There had been substantial changes – almost a revolution – in real warfare, due to the lessons learnt by Edward III during his Scottish wars. A combination of defensive position and the use of Welsh archers and knights fighting on foot was the outcome: instead of relying on the force of cavalry charges, Edward, the Black Prince and their leading commanders took the view that if a strong enough position could be found, the opposing cavalry would

Tournaments

The Treatise on the Form and Scheme of a Tournament, *written by René, duke of Anjou, in the latter years of his life, is one of the most spectacular witnesses to the splendour of these occasions. René was one of the most enthusiastic tourneyers of his age, and he was also a great patron of the arts. The resulting manuscript portrays a kind of ideal tournament, rather than a specific occasion, and he incorporates German and Flemish customs as well as the ancient French ways, which he sees as the true original tradition. The pages that follow show the dukes of Bourbon and Brittany in full tourneying panoply, the opening of the tournament with both sides drawn up ready for the marshals to cut the ropes, and the furious action of the mêlée. Finally, we see the victor of the tournament being awarded his prize at the dance which followed such an event.*

Knights hang out their banners at their lodgings before a tournament

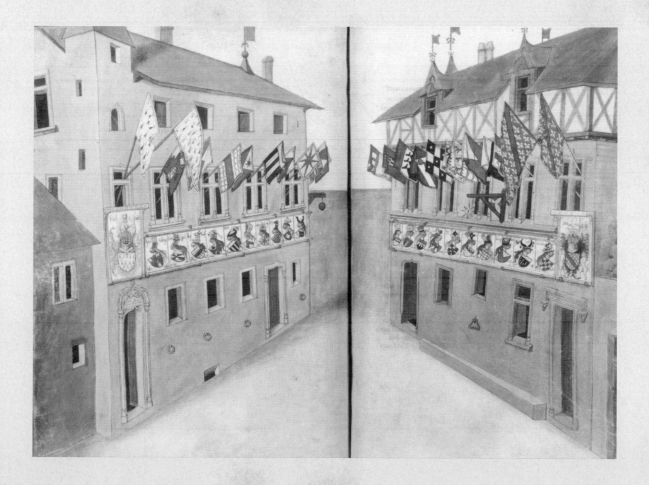

The Dukes of Brittany and Bourbon armed for a tournament, from René d'Anjou's treatise on tournaments

The start of a tournament, from René d'Anjou's treatise on tournaments

The mêlée with swords, from René d'Anjou's treatise on tournaments

The presentation of prizes after a tournament, from René d'Anjou's treatise on tournaments

wear themselves out before they broke the defensive line, particularly in view of the damage done by the archers. In any case, the archers (and likewise cannon, used for the first time in battle at Crécy in 1346) were not equipped to mount an attack. There was a further factor as well: during the Middle Ages very few armies which launched an attack on an enemy fighting on the defensive were victorious. It is an open question as to how far medieval commanders studied tactics, but the point may well have played a part in Edward's changes in his method of warfare.

Let us see how these tactics worked in practice. At Crécy on 26 August 1346, Edward had been expecting an attack by the French under King Philip for some days. The English army had been in the field for over a month, and had marched from the far side of Normandy to Picardy; Edward could not expect to outmarch his adversary's fresh troops. So the advantage was with

*The effigy of the Black
Prince in Canterbury
Cathedral portrays him
as the ideal chivalric hero*

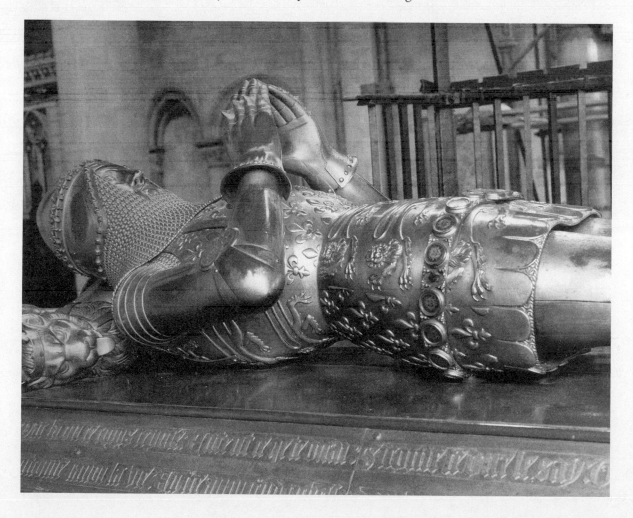

Philip. Edward chose a defensive position outside the forest of Crécy, at the top of a small hill; he arranged his troops in three battles, two of which, with groups of archers interspersed, formed the front line. The English army was in position by early morning: the knights dismounted, and their horses were put in a kind of *laager* of carts behind the army. In front of the army, pits were dug to break the French charge, a technique learnt from the Scots.

The French army arrived on the scene in the late afternoon – or rather, the first part of it did. A medieval army on the march spread out over a considerable distance, often several miles, and Philip should have regrouped his forces before attacking. However, even while his scouts reported that the English were well entrenched and a halt should be called until the next morning, the French vanguard, confident of victory, had come up close to the English. They now had to be not merely halted but actually recalled, and this they either failed or refused to do. The French army had been assembled only a week or two earlier, and had no experience of working together; it included troops from Flanders, Germany and Bohemia, as well as hired crossbowmen from Genoa. These last were the first to go into action, and they quickly discovered that the English archers, whom they had never faced in battle before, had an equally good range and a far superior rate of fire. The primitive cannons added to their discomfiture and they turned to flee. But the French column immediately behind them thought that this was treachery, and instead of waiting until the way was clear before charging, simply rode them down.

Not surprisingly, this first charge was fairly ineffective, and the leader of this column, the Duc d'Alençon, was killed with many of his men. The second French column now came up and succeeded in pressing home their attack, although many of their horses were killed by the English archers. However, the Black Prince and his men had the better of the hand-to-hand fighting, even though they had to ask the King to send reinforcements from the reserve. Among the dead was King John of Bohemia, one of the great warriors of the age who, although old and blind, had ordered his attendants to take him into the thick of the battle. The French continued to charge the English line, but as the ground became more and more obstructed by bodies and dead horses the impact of the charges diminished; the survivors of each charge fled, leaving only King Philip and a small group of footsoldiers, who left the battlefield at nightfall when the last attacks had failed.

The French losses were relatively high, some 1542 men-at-arms and knights out of an army with at most 12,000 mounted men in it. The English, on the other hand, lost very few men. The English archers must have accounted for a large number of the dead, but the lack of discipline of the French was also a contributory factor: one knight on the English side is reported to have been killed 'charging recklessly into the battle-line', and, by and large the French assaults consisted of groups of knights being equally reckless and failing to break through the well-prepared English defences. In a tournament or an old-fashioned cavalry battle, impetus was everything; even a single knight charging with great force into a group of horsemen might make a considerable impression. Faced with an army in a position designed to break such an impetus, co-ordination was all-important: the French might have won if they had succeeded in riding down the English archers rather than their own crossbowmen, but such tactical subtleties were beyond the scope of an army which went into action virtually on the march.

Some of the lessons of Crécy were learnt in the following decade, but the French were once again heavily defeated at Poitiers. There, King John had a much clearer tactical plan. The first mounted charge by the French was to destroy the Black Prince's archers; a second wave, on foot, would then break up the English formation, which would be overwhelmed by the two succeeding battles. The French army was numerically superior, and the English were weary from a month's campaigning. Why then did the French plan fail? The main reason was once again indiscipline. The first charge, led by two marshals of France, was marred by disputes between the commanders, and failed to achieve its objective because they insisted on attacking the wings independently. In fairness, it was a difficult task, as the Black Prince had placed the archers in swamps and woods where cavalry would have difficulty reaching them. The French knights in the main army disliked the idea fighting on foot, and this manoeuvre was in any case a misconception: to send knights in heavy armour toiling across fields in the heat of day was not the way to deliver a strong attack. Dismounted knights fought very effectively in defensive positions; on the offensive, however, dismounting offered no advantage. Furthermore, the morale of French knights was undermined by this strange method of fighting, and when the first dismounted attack failed, the second battle simply rode off the field without striking a blow, leaving the King's division to attack alone. The Prince now remounted his men and delivered a counter-attack; a detachment took the French in the rear. This encircling movement sealed their fate, and despite a desperate resistance, King John was captured.

In essence, the English victories were due to the fact that they made best possible use of their resources, while the French squandered theirs. Yet the French had the reputation of being the best knights in Europe. The paradox points to a fundamental failure in knightly training. Discipline played a relatively minor part in the knight's ideals, while individual glory was the essence of his existence. The French army was a group of individuals, while the English knights subordinated their chivalric ideals to military needs. There were of course exceptions: at Poitiers, as at Crécy, single knights left the English lines to find death or glory. More typical than this handful of disobedient enthusiasts was Sir James Audley, who indulged his knightly desire for glory only at the end of the battle; when the Prince had decided to charge, Audley begged to be allowed to lead it, and was severely wounded as a result.

The French armies had much less experience of routine military action, whereas the English forces were turned into seasoned troops by their experience as raiders. These 'chevauchées' were as important as set battles or sieges, even though much less glamorous. Five major expeditions of this kind were undertaken in Edward III's reign: to Normandy 1346; the Black Prince's raid in south-west France in 1355; the Poitiers expedition of 1356; the Rheims campaign of 1359–60; and John Gaunt's raid in 1373. The object of such raids was twofold: to damage the economic base of the French war-effort and to terrify the local population into changing allegiance to the English. Two extracts from campaign diaries will illustrate how a raid worked. The first describes Edward III's army on the march at the beginning of the campaign that ended with the battle of Crécy:

The English, eager to make war on the enemy, ranged across various parts of the country on the 14th [of July, 1346], and several reached the town of Barfleur, where they found an abundance of hidden riches and returned unharmed with a number of prisoners, both citizens and peasants. But they first burnt the town, and seven curiously fitted-out warships as well, which they found in the port. The army ravaged in a similar fashion on the 15th, 16th and 17th; the English King appointed the Earl of Northampton constable, and the Earl of Warwick marshal of the army, to check the rashness of the troops. Then they organised the army into three divisions: the vanguard under the Prince of Wales, the centre under the King, and the rearguard under the Bishop of Durham. With the army divided in this way by the King's counsel, and with everything prepared in the correct fashion, the King began his journey into Normandy on the 18th of July. By thickly wooded and very narrow roads, the army reached the town of Valognes, a rich and worthy place, without harm or mishap. The inhabitants of the town came out and threw themselves at the King's feet, asking him only to spare their lives; the King most mercifully admitted them to his peace. The King lodged in the house of the Dukes of Normandy, while the Prince stayed in the house of the Bishop of Coutances.

On the 19th, some evildoers who were not afraid of breaking the King's edict left the army, and set fire to everything near the road. The English army left the fine town of Montebourg to one side, and unharnessed at Saint Côme du Mont. Here they heard rumours that [the bridge nearby] had been broken down by the retreating enemy, hoping to hinder the King's progress. The causeway was narrow and the water very deep, too deep to ford. Nor could the King find any other place for his army to cross: so he put Reginald Cobham, John Stirling, Roger Mortimer, Hugh Despenser and Bartholomew de Burghersh the younger in charge of the bridge and causeway, so that both could be repaired and strengthened as necessary by the carpenters.

On the 20th, the King and his army crossed the bridge and causeway safely, and came to the town of Carentan, surrounded by strong moats and marshes, and embellished by a fairly strong castle, but the footsoldiers who had gone on ahead devoured a large amount of food, regardless of danger and ignoring the harm it might do to the army. It was very strictly ordered in the King's name that no one should waste more food than he needed. After they had crossed the bridge, leaving the island of Saint-Marcouf behind, they now reached the borders of Normandy. The King and his army crossed four bridges in the marsh already mentioned, and followed a narrow causeway. They pitched their tents at Pont-Hebert, after a longer day's journey than usual. The bridge into Normandy, broken down by the retreating enemy, was repaired by the Prince of Wales that day, but no one was able to cross it until the morning; when all the vanguard was to go over: for the King had heard that Robert Bertram and others of the enemy were not far from his army, and did not want to lose any of his men while they could be defended. The vanguard crossed on the 22nd and climbed to the top of a nearby hill, and drew themselves up in battle array against a possible enemy attack which, they hoped, was imminent. Here Henry de Burghersh was knighted by the Prince of Wales. These lords entered St Lô, a walled town with a castle, together that night, where there was plenty of food of all kinds. The Constable and Marshal of France and others of the enemy had sheltered here the previous night. At the dawn trumpet-call on the 23rd, the King ordered the army to gather at Torigni, but new information reached him, and he suddenly changed his plans and set out in a different direction, to Cormolain. The enemy had also been here the previous night. Those who were responsible for quartering the English army at Torigni, reserving houses for the nobles, learnt of the army's retreat and, setting fire to town and countryside, hastened to the King, coming in small groups from all over the countryside.

Nine years later the Prince embarked on a similar expedition in south-western France, described in a letter from his steward, Sir John Wingfield, to the Bishop of Winchester, administrator of the Prince's English estates:

My lord, as to news from these parts, you will be glad to know that my lord the Prince and all the earls, barons, bannerets, knights and squires were in good health when this was written. And my lord has not lost any knights or squires on this expedition except for Sir John Lisle who was killed, very strangely, by a crossbow bolt on the third day after we entered enemy territory; and he died on 15 October. And, my lord, you will be glad to know that my lord has raided the county of Armagnac and taken several walled towns there, burning and destroying them, except for certain towns which he garrisoned. Then he went into the viscounty of Rivière, and took a good town called Plaisance, the chief town of the area, and burnt it and laid waste the surrounding countryside. Then he went into the county of Astarac, and took several towns and had them burnt and destroyed, and the countryside likewise, and took the chief town, called Samatan, which is as large as Norwich. Then he entered the county of Lisle and took some of the walled towns and had a number of good towns through which he passed burnt and destroyed. Then he entered the lordship of Toulouse, and we crossed the river Garonne and another a mile upstream of Toulouse, which is very large, because our enemy had broken all the bridges on both sides of Toulouse, except for the bridges in Toulouse, because the river goes through the town. The Constable of France, the Marshal de Clermont and the Count of Armagnac were in the town at the time, with a great army. And the town of Toulouse is very large, strong and fine, and well fortified. And there was no one in our army who knew where the ford was, but by God's grace we found it. And then he went through the lordship of Toulouse and took several good walled towns and burnt and destroyed them, laying waste the surrounding countryside. And then we entered the lordship of Carcassonne and took several good towns before we came to Carcassonne; and he took Carcassonne, which is larger, stronger and finer than York. And all that town and all the other towns in the region were burnt and destroyed. And then we marched for some days until we had crossed the Carcassonne region and entered the lordship of Narbonne: and we took several towns, and laid them waste, until we came to Narbonne. And the town of Narbonne resisted us and was taken by assault. The said town is only a little smaller than London, and is on the Mediterranean, from which it is only separated by about eight miles. And there is a harbour and landing place, and the river comes into Narbonne. And Narbonne is only sixty miles from Montpellier, seventy from Aigues-Mortes and a hundred and twenty from Avignon. You will be glad to know that the Holy Father sent his envoys to my lord, who were only thirty miles away from him. And the envoys sent a sergeant-at-arms, who was sergeant-at-arms at the Pope's chamber door, with letters from them to my lord, asking for safe conduct to come to my lord, setting out their mission from the Pope, which was to negotiate between my lord and his French adversaries. And the messenger was with the army for two days before my lord would see him or receive his letters. The reason was that my lord had news that the French army had come out of Toulouse towards Carcassonne, and my lord wanted to turn back on them suddenly; and so did. And on the third day, when we should have attacked them, they had news of our movement before daybreak; and they retreated and disappeared towards the mountains and fastnesses, and returned to Toulouse in long marches. The local people who acted as their guides when they went that way left them, and were captured as they returned home. And because the Pope's sergeant-at-arms was in my custody, I made him question the guides who were captured; for the guide whom he questioned was the guide of the Constable of France, a native of the country, and he could know and recognize that they were Frenchmen by questioning them. And I told the sergeant that he could go and report to the Pope and the rest of them at Avignon what he had seen and heard. And as for my lord's reply to the envoys, you would be delighted to hear the whole story. For he refused to let the envoys come a step closer; but if they wanted to negotiate, they were to send to my lord the King, and my lord would do nothing except by the order of the King, nor. would he listen to any proposals without his command. As to my lord's return in pursuit of his enemy, and the crossing of the Garonne, and the capture of castles and towns on the way, and the other things he did to the enemy as he pursued them, all of which was well and honourably done, as many know and Sir Richard Stafford and Sir William Burton will be able to explain in full, I cannot describe this in a letter, as it would take too long. My lord was in the field against his enemies for eight weeks and only took eleven rest days. It seems certain that since the war against the French King began, there has never been such destruction in a region as in this raid. For the countryside and towns which have been destroyed in this raid produced more revenue for the King of France in aid of his wars than half his kingdom; and that is without the profits of recoinage and the profits and customs which he takes from those of Poitou, as I could prove from authentic documents found in various towns in the tax-collectors' houses. For Carcassonne and Limoux, which is as large as Carcassonne, and two other towns near there, produce for the King of France each year the wages of a thousand men at arms and 100,000 old crowns towards the costs of the war. According to the records which we found, the towns around Toulouse, Carcassonne and Narbonne which we destroyed, together with Narbonne itself, produced each year, over and above this, 400,000 old crowns as war subsidies; and the citizens of the larger towns and other inhabitants, who should know about such matters, have told us this. And, by God's help, if my lord had money to continue this war and to profit the King and his honour, he could indeed enlarge the boundaries of his territory' and take a number of places, because the enemy are in great disarray. In order to do this my lord has ordered all the earls and bannerets to stay in different places along the border in order to raid and damage the enemy's lands. My lord, that is all the news for, the moment, but please write to me and let me know your wishes, and I will do my best to help. Most honoured lord, may God send you long life, joy and good health. Written at Bordeaux, Wednesday before Christmas.

Raids like these were organised on a substantial scale, and were often intended to draw the enemy out to give battle, as well as achieve economic and political ends. In the case of Crécy and Poitiers, object was attained, but the

French grew wary thereafter: Charles changed his strategy to a war of attrition, which the English, far from their home bases, could not hope to win. The Rheims campaign ended in stalemate, that of 1373 in near-disaster: the armies marched unopposed through France but suffered severely from shortage of provisions and bad weather.

At an even humbler level was the everyday border warfare of minor raids which went on throughout the Anglo-French wars, ranging from the taking of a castle to a skirmish between two small groups of knights or merely the burning of an enemy village. In this atmosphere, lawless elements came into their own, and the so-called free companies grew up. Their leaders might call themselves knights, but they were usually unpaid mercenary men-at-arms who, when their pay was not forthcoming, had taken to freebooting. Yet warfare for many ordinary knights was not very different from what the companies did – ravaging, looting, skirmishing – and knights whose own lands had been ravaged were often forced to take up this kind of existence. In Germany in the mid-fifteenth century the Westphalian lords had 'fields unfruitful that they lie as desert, uncultivated ... you could not watch without tears the way in which these fine knights had to fight, day in, day out, for their food and clothing, and risked the gallows or the wheel in order to avoid hunger and want.'

But even in the most prosaic siege or raid, knights could still find opportunities for chivalric action; indeed, in small-scale actions, such deeds were more likely to be noticed and were less foolhardy than in a pitched battle. Here is Froissart's description of such a skirmish, at the siege of Hennebont in 1342. Sir Walter Manny has just arrived from England to help the Countess of Montfort, and finds the besieged much troubled by a siege machine, which was bombarding the town incessantly with large stones:

After the entertainment, Sir Walter Manny, who was captain of the English, inquired of the countess the state of the town and of the enemy's army. Upon looking out of the window he said he had a great inclination to destroy that large machine which was placed so near, and much annoyed them, if any would second him. Sir Yves de Tresiquidi replied that he would not fail him in this his first expedition; as did also the Lord of Landreman. They went to arm themselves, and then sallied quietly out of one of the gates, taking with them three hundred archers, who shot so well, that those who guarded the machine fled; and the men-at-arms who followed the archers, falling upon them, slew the greater part, and broke down and cut in pieces this large machine. They then dashed in among the tents and huts, set fire to them, and killed and wounded many of their enemies before the army was in motion. After this they made a handsome retreat. When the

During the tedium of long sieges, knights sought distraction by arranging duels with the enemy, separated by barriers

enemy were mounted and armed, they galloped after them like madmen. Sir Walter Manny, seeing this, exclaimed, 'May I never be embraced by my mistress and dear friend, if I enter castle or fortress before I have unhorsed one of these gallopers.' He then turned round, and pointed his spear towards the enemy, as did the two brothers of Lande-Halle, le Haze de Brabant, Sir Yves de Tresiquidi, Sir Galeran de Landreman, and many others, and spitted the first coursers. Many legs were made to kick the air. Some of their own party were also unhorsed. The conflict became very serious, for reinforcements were perpetually coming from the camp; and the English were obliged to retreat towards the castle, which they did in good order until they came to the castle ditch: there the knights made a stand, until all their men were safely returned. Many brilliant actions, captures, and rescues might have been seen. Those of the town who had not been of the party to destroy the large machine now sued forth, and, ranging themselves upon the banks of the ditch, made such good use of their bows, that they forced the enemy to withdraw, killing many men and horses. The chiefs of the army, realising they had the worst of it, and that they were losing men to no purpose, sounded a retreat, and made their men retire to the camp. As soon as they were gone, the townsmen re-entered, and sent each to his quarters. The Countess of Montfort came down from the castle to meet them, and with a most cheerful countence, kissed Sir Walter Manny, and all his companions, one after the other, like a noble and valiant dame.

But even such diversions as these disappeared in the following century. Sieges became the business of gunners, and it was rather less easy to destroy a cannon than a wooden siege-engine. Nor was armour any longer a sufficient defence against such weapons. By the mid-fifteenth century, the French had built up a considerable artillery force, which played an important part in their reconquest of Normandy in 1449–50, enabling the French to batter their way into the strongest fortresses with remarkable ease, and which also determined the outcome of the battle of Formigny in 1450. In 1453, the commander of the English forces in France, Sir John Talbot, was killed by a cannon-ball at Castillon-sur-Dordogne when he rashly tried to attack an entrenched artillery position. The knight's domination had come to an end: indeed, the last major victory to be won by a cavalry charge was at Roosebeke in 1382, where Charles VI and his knights overran a Flemish infantry force who had no archers among them. Even against the Turkish light horsemen in the East, the Western cavalry was ineffective: a crusading army was overwhelmed at Nicopolis in 1396, partly out of excessive enthusiasm and lack of discipline, partly because the superior speed of the Turkish horse enabled them to withdraw in the face of each charge, until the heavier Western horses were exhausted. At Tannenberg in 1410, the knights of the Teutonic Order used a mixture of light horse and heavily-armed knights, but were overwhelmed by a numerically superior army of Poles and Lithuanians.

Fifteenth-century battles by and large show a very different pattern from those of the earlier Middle Ages. The three great defeats suffered by Charles the Bold of Burgundy, at Grandson, Morten and Nancy, were all the result of his inferior tactics, so that his army was either partially or completely unprepared. Even at Nancy, where he had drawn up his army in battle order, the Duke of Lorraine and his Swiss allies were able to surprise him by a flanking movement out of view of his scouts. The main weapon of the Swiss was the pike, but their armies also contained archers and cavalry, and their tactics were not strikingly novel. For new developments; we have to look further afield, to Bohemia, where the armies of the religious dissidents known as Hussites developed the use of handguns and defensive waggons formed; 'laagers', a much more sophisticated version of the tactic used by Edward III at Crécy. The handgun was soon to replace the bow missile weapon of the infantry, and once again the knight was the loser for armour was no protection against a hail of bullets.

Another fifteenth-century development cut at the basis of chivalry. The knight was in a sense a paid soldier – 'the fief is the pay of the knight' – but the method of payment and his terms of service made discipline by means of withdrawal of pay impossible to enforce; his fief was hereditary, a possession at law, and the terms of service we limited by custom or agreement. In 1445, Charles VII introduced the Compagnies d'Ordonnance in France, twenty companies of six hundred men each, employed full-time as soldiers and paid in cash, not kind. This, the first standing army in Europe since Roman times, meant that the knights could no longer claim to be the professional elite of warriors, but were replaced by the successors to their old competitors the mercenary soldiers.

As the knight's role in warfare diminished, so the tournament became less and less concerned with being a replica of war, and became more and more a pure pageant and social occasion, a way of proclaiming the wealth and power of a prince rather than of training his fighting men. The tournament as pageant reached its apogee in the splendid festivals organised by René d'Anjou and the Burgundian dukes. This, however, was no great innovation, but what was a novelty was the increasing use of elaborate dramatic scenarios as settings for the tournament as a whole. There had been an element of disguise and costume in tournaments since the late thirteenth century; by 1428, when Philip the Good of Burgundy sent ambassadors to Portugal, they were entertained by jousts with the outline of a dramatic setting:

At this supper, which lasted a long time, certain entertainments took place which they call challenges. They happen like this. Knights and gentlemen, fully armed and equipped for jousting, enter on horseback accompanied as they please and approach the table where the lord or lady giving the feast is seated. Without dismounting, the knight bows and presents to his host a letter or piece of paper, fixed to a stick split at the end, in which it is stated that he is a knight or gentleman with such and such a name, which he had chosen, and that he comes from some strange land, such as 'the deserts of India', 'terrestrial paradise', 'the sea', or 'the land', to seek adventures. Because he has heard about this magnificent feast, he has come to court, and he now declares that he is ready to receive anyone present who wishes to perform a deed of arms with him. When the letter has been read out and the thing discussed, the host causes a herald to say to the gentleman, who is awaiting a reply in front of the table: 'Knight, or lord, you shall be delivered.' Then, bowing again as before, he leaves, armed and mounted as before. One came all covered in spines, both he and his horse, like a porcupine. Another came accompanied by the seven planets, each nicely portrayed according to its special characteristics. Several others came elegantly dressed and disguised, each as he chose...

Next day, 27 September, after dinner, there was jousting in the Rua Nova in Lisbon, which was spread with a great deal of sand. There was a fence of stakes fixed into the ground at intervals, to joust along, which was hung with blue and vermilion woollen cloths. Some of the jousters came with their horses adorned wit cloth-of-gold, embroidered and fur-lined; others were decked out in cloth embroidered with silver, or silk cloth... and they jousted magnificently in front of the King and the lords and ladies who watched them from the windows of houses along the street. On the next day, 28 September, likewise, solemn and impressive jousts were held there.

By the sixteenth century, the stray knights 'in character' had become the cast of a play. At jousts held at Binche in Flanders in 1549, in honour of Philip II of Spain, the tournament became the 'Adventure the Castle Tenebrous', carefully arranged to glorify the King. It began with a feast at which a knight errant appeared and explained how an enchanter had imprisoned certain ladies, who could be freed only if a magic sword could be drawn from its sheath. A series of prepared adventures, complete with stage-effects and interspersed with jousting followed, most of the incidents being drawn from romances, culminating with the drawing of the magic sword – by Philip himself of course – and the freeing of the prisoners. This festival had obvious political overtones, being centred on the person of the King; others, such as René d'Anjou's *Pas d'armes de la bergière* held at Tarascon in 1449, had less serious matters in mind. At Tarascon, René's mistress, dressed as a shepherdess and with a real flock of sheep, was the focal point of the festivities: two knights fought on her behalf, one representing happiness in love, the other sorrow in love, and the challengers chose their opponent according to the state of their heart. Those content in love to fought the sorrowful knight of the black shield, while the discontented fought the cheerful knight bearing a white shield. The poet who described the scene had to admit that the illusion was not entirely successful: 'the knights scarcely looked like shepherds because of their armour'. And indeed the very idea of a pastoral tournament – martial alarums disguised as rural peace – is a contradiction in terms, and an indication of how unreal the world of knightly warfare had become.

Chivalry and Literature

T he knight as warrior is no different from the epic heroes of battlefields of other ages. The magic spell which transmutes mere knighthood into chivalry is that of courtly love; and that spell was, appropriately, the work of poets and writers of romance. The apogee of the knight as fighting man – and hence as hero – coincided with the first flowering of a literature in everyday language. Up to the twelfth century, most literature had been written in Latin, except in outlandish places like Saxon England. Now poets began to explore the possibilities of ordinary, everyday language, and in France between 1120 and 1170 there was a flowering of poetry and prose all the more remarkable because it seemed so sudden. In fact, the suddenness of the appearance of the new literature is partly an illusion: the poets drew on older, lost material, some of it spoken, some of it taken from other civilisations. But what concerns us is that just as tournaments and a concept of knighthood were developing, so poets were creating a new literary world, which complemented them, moving beyond the simple epic celebration of heroism in war to a complex interplay of deeds and emotions. In the same way that the tournament was a kind of artificial, sophisticated warfare, so the new romances were also artificial and sophisticated in their analysis of feeling.

There are, broadly speaking, four elements in the great medieval romances of chivalry, and to trace the way in which chivalry as a literary ideal developed, we must take each in turn. They are: heroism or prowess (the epic), love (the lyric), marvels (the folktale), and the romance form itself, centring on both hero and heroine. In literary terms, the epic is the oldest of the four forms, going back to the Near Eastern poems of Gilgamesh and of the Bible, and to

Homer's *Iliad* and *Odyssey*. The foremost ingredient of the epic is action: the epic hero's worth is measured by his victories, his escapes from impossible odds, his defiance of ordinary human limitations. The basic principle of the epic is that certain men were to be regarded, in Maurice Bowra's words, 'as a generation of superior beings who sought and deserved honour'. The Greeks were by no means alone in this; Bowra points out epic poems from Russia, Eastern Europe, the Far East and Africa, in which similar principles and even similar episodes may be found, ranging in date from the third millennium BC to the twentieth century. The poems with which we are concerned, however, are more limited in range. The two European epics which are most representative of the heroic poetry which a twelfth-century knight – or poet – would have known, are the *Chanson de Roland* from France and the *Cantar del Mio Cid* from Spain.

Roland fights Ferragut: a twelfth century carving of a scene from the Chanson de Roland, the greatest of the French medieval epics

The *Chanson de Roland* is the foremost and earliest example of poems known as *chansons de geste*, 'songs of deeds', which may have originated in contemporary songs celebrating great feats of arms, but which (in the form they have come down to us) are always written about historic or pseudo-historic characters. This distancing in time makes the mood of the poems faintly nostalgic, as well as providing the essential excuse for suspension of disbelief, that things were different in those far-off days. The Greeks looked back to an heroic age, described by Hesiod in his *Works and Days*:

Again on the bountiful earth by heaven was sent
A worthier race; on righteous deeds they were bent,
 Divine, heroic – as demigods they are known,
And the boundless earth had their race before our own.
Some of them met grim war and its battle fates:
In the land of Kadmos at Thebes with seven gates
They fought for Oedipus' flocks disastrously,
Or were drawn to cross the gulf of mighty sea
For sake of Helen tossing her beautiful hair,
And death was the sudden shroud that wrapped them there.

In the *chansons de geste* it is the age of Charlemagne that is the setting for heroic deeds, some three hundred years before the lifetimes of the poets. But in both cases there is a core of historical fact. Archaeology has brought to light the real world of Hesiod's heroes, while Charlemagne's paladins are to be found, even if obscurely, in the history books. Einhard, writing a biography of Charlemagne in about 830, tells how in 778 Charlemagne was returning across the Pyrenees from a Spanish expedition, when:

. . . he was given a taste of Basque treachery. Dense forests, which stretch in all directions, make this a spot most suitable for setting ambushes. At a moment when Charlemagne's army was stretched out in a long column of march, as the nature of the local defiles forced it to be, these Basques, who had set their ambush on the very top of one of the mountains, came rushing down on the last part of the baggage train and the troops who were marching in support of the rearguard and so protecting the army which had gone on ahead. The Basques forced them down into the valley beneath, joined battle with them and killed them to the last man. They then snatched up the baggage and, protected as they were by the cover of darkness, which was just beginning to fall, scattered in all directions without losing a moment. In this feat the Basques were helped by the lightness of their arms and by the nature of the terrain in which the battle was fought. On the other hand, the heavy nature of their own equipment and the unevenness of the ground completely hampered the Franks in their resistance to the Basques. In this battle died Eggihard, who was in charge of the King's table, Anshelm, the Count of the Palace, and Roland, Lord of the Breton Marches, along with a great number of others.

This brief entry becomes a poem of four thousand lines in the *Chanson de Roland*: Eggihard and Anshelm vanish, but two important characters are added, the traitor Ganelon and Roland's faithful comrade Oliver, and there are many minor embellishments of detail. But the core of the poem remains the action at the unnamed place of ambush, which the poet identifies as the pass of Roncevaux. The first thousand lines form a prelude, telling how Ganelon arranged for Roland to be chosen for the rearguard and then treacherously arranged for the 'paynim' to attack him. The description of the battle occupies

Servants pitch a tent on campaign, from the Chanson de Roland

nearly fifteen hundred lines, Charlemagne's revenge and a further great battle in which the slayers of Roland are defeated take another quarter of the poem, and Ganelon's death rounds off the story in a mere three hundred lines.

The emphasis of the poem, then, is simple: it is a poem about one man's conduct in battle. Its ideals are loyalty to lord and friend and country: Charlemagne, Oliver and France are foremost in Roland's mind. There is a heroine, *'la belle Aude'*, Roland's betrothed, but her part is only to swoon and die when she hears of Roland's death – Roland spares no thought for her during the battle. Individual emotion is in fact subservient to the greater ends of empire and Christianity. Roland's death occurs slightly over halfway through the poem, and does not strike us as a tragedy. The larger framework is Charlemagne's struggle against the Saracens in Spain, in which Roland's heroic death is an episode, part of a setback which is avenged by the Emperor's triumphant capture of Saragossa. The poem ends with a reminder that the struggle against paganism and evil cannot be won by a single campaign: the Archangel Gabriel appears to Charlemagne and tells him of a new appeal for help from a beleaguered Christian king.

Yet if the framework looks beyond the individual, the actual events of the poem are concentrated on one or two figures at a time, usually pairs of knights locked in combat. Even here, there is strict discipline and a sense of military decorum: Roland does not charge recklessly into the thick of the enemy, but meets each Saracen onslaught as it comes. The mood is that of the Frankish infantry at Poitiers in 733: 'motionless as a wall, and frozen together like a block of ice, they put the Arabs to the sword.' As the enemy attack, one or two of the Frankish lords ride out to avenge their fallen comrades, and it is these combats that are the highlight of the poem. One can imagine a knightly audience spellbound by such a recital, each man identifying with the Frankish protagonists. Here, in Dorothy Sayers' rather stilted yet often powerful translation, is one of these encounters:

> There was a Paynim, and Grandoyne was he called,
> King Capuel's son, from Cappadocia's shores,
> Mounted on Marmor, for so he names his horse,
> Swifter of speed than any bird that soars.
> He slacks the rein and he goes spurring forth,
> And runs to strike Gèrin with all his force.
> From off his neck he splits the red shield shorn,

From off his body he rips the byrny torn,
Into his heart the pennon blue he's borne,
And down he flings him dead on a rocky tor.
Gèrin his comrade he smites down afterward,
Berenger next, Guy of St Antoine fall;
And then he strikes the mighty duke Astorge,
(Envers-on-Rhone and Valence called him lord),
And lays him dead; for joy the Paynims roar;
The French all say: 'What loss we have to mourn!'

The County Roland grips fast his blood-red blade;
Well has he heard how the French are dismayed;
His heart grieves so, 'tis like to split in twain.
He hails the Paynim: 'God send thee all His plagues!
Thou hast slain one for whom I'll make thee pay!'
He spurs his horse that gladly runs apace;
Let win who may, they're at it, face to face.
The Prince Grandoyne was a good knight and gallant,
Strong of his hands and valorous in battle;
Athwart him now comes Roland the great captain;
He'd never met him, but he knew him instanter.
By his proud aspect, and by his noble stature,
His haughty looks, and his bearing and manner.
He cannot help it, a mortal fear unmans him;
Fain would he fly, but what's the good? he cannot.
The count assails him with such ferocious valour
That to the nasal the whole helmet is shattered,
Cloven the nose and the teeth and the palate,
The jaz'rain hauberk and the breastbone and backbone,
Both silver bows from off the golden saddle;
Horseman and horse clean asunder he slashes,
Lifeless he leaves them and the pieces past patching.
The men of Spain fall a-wailing for sadness:
The French all cry: 'What strokes! and what a champion!'

When Roland sounds his great war-horn, or Olifant, with the last of his
strength, its sound reaches Charlemagne far ahead in the van of the army,

and the Emperor and his men at once turn back, full of anxiety for their comrades:

> *Huge are the hills and shadowy and high,*
> *Deep in the vales the living streams run by.*
> *The trumpets sound before them and behind,*
> *All with one voice to Olifant reply.*
> *In wrath of heart the Emperor Carlon rides,*
> *And all the French in sorrow and in ire;*
> *There's none but grieves and weeps from out his eyes;*
> *They all pray God to safeguard Roland's life*
> *Till they may come to battle by his side;*
> *Once they are with him they'll make it a great fight.*
> *What use is that? their prayers are empty quite,*
> *Too long they've lingered, they cannot come in time.*

Loyalty, comradeship and prowess are the knight's great virtues: their counterparts are treachery, faithlessness and cowardice, and just as Roland is perfect, so nothing good can be said of the traitor Ganelon. Even his noble birth seems a kind of reproach, making his abasement all the more acute. It is a black and white world of absolutes, powerfully described.

With the poem on the Spanish hero Rodrigo Diaz de Vivar, known as the Cid, we are in a more complicated situation. The Cid was again an historical character, but he belonged to the recent past when the poems about him were composed. Instead of a gap of two centuries between deeds and poem, there was perhaps as little as fifty years. So the portrait of the Cid is infinitely more realistic. It has been suggested that the *Chanson de Roland* was influenced by the First Crusade in 1099; and there is certainly an idealised crusading ring to the battles between Franks and Saracens. The Cid is portrayed as fighting a much more down-to-earth war, probably because such warfare was still familiar to the poet, who did not see it as a great cause but as a fact of everyday life.

So we find scenes of domestic pathos in the Cid's parting from his wife, and the poet underlines the hero's concern to provide his daughters with suitable dowries and husbands – which he does by defeating the Moors at Valencia and then marrying his daughters to the kings of Aragon and Navarre. The poet's feeling is still heroic, but he is in touch with the ordinary affairs of a knight. The Cid, too, is no scion of a noble stock like Roland; he is a humble landowner, with a small estate, and makes his way as an adventurer. When he is exiled through his enemies' scheming, he does not hesitate to go into Moorish service, and his very name reflects this: it is the Arabic *sidi*, lord.

The *Cantar del Mio Cid* is in many ways nearer to the verse biography of William Marshal in its faithful reporting of historical reality overlaid with a desire to commemorate a great warrior. Just as this poem is very different in style from the abstract heroism of the *Chanson de Roland*, so Spanish chivalry took a very different form from the French: in the fourteenth century Froissart complained that the Spaniards mistreated knights whom they took prisoner, loading them with chains to extort the maximum ransom, while in the fifteenth century both real knights, such as Gutierrez Diaz de Gamez, and the imaginary knights of romance indulged in exploits more fantastic than their French counterparts. In a curious way this may have been due to the long-drawn-out war of the Reconquista, which only ended with the fall of the Moorish kingdom of Granada in 1492. Chivalry and real war became separated in Spain, whereas in France they were – often disastrously – entangled.

*Charlemagne sets out
with his army: from the
Chanson de Roland*

Germany, with its different traditions drawn from the Norse world, has little to offer in the way of epic poetry. The one apparent epic, the *Nibelungenlied*, brings us to the borders of epic and romance. It has some ingredients of pure epic – a strongly delineated hero in Siegfried, roots in the history of fifth-century Burgundy, the same bonds of loyalty as in the *Chanson de Roland*. In versions now lost to us, the story must have once been an epic pure and simple. But it has become overlaid with both folktale, in the figure of the tamed hero-maiden Brunhild, won by magic, and with later romantic ideas, in the handling of the plot and the attitude to women. In many ways the most interesting figure is not Siegfried – who also has his share of folktale characteristics – but the 'villain', Hagen, who kills Siegfried out of fanatical loyalty to his master King Gunther. The twelfth-century poet who recast the story has emasculated it at certain points, and so removed it yet further from its epic original. In the original, Siegfried not only wins Brunhild for the King but, against his agreement with Gunther, sleeps with her. This treason is repaid by Hagen's treacherous murder which Siegfried's wife Kriemhild avenges in turn by killing Hagen: a simple pattern of vengeance and revenge. In the *Nibelungenlied*, after Siegfried has fought Brunhild and forced her to submit, he merely takes her ring and girdle, and Gunther at once changes places with him and lies with her. The effect of chivalric taste here is to produce a less coherent and convincing tale, and to weaken its inner drive without offering a new set of motives in its place.

With hindsight, the obvious solution to the problem facing the poet of the *Nibelungenlied* would have been to reshape it into a drama of courtly love, Siegfried perhaps playing the part of Lancelot to Brunhild's Guinevere. But before we explore the second branch, that of love and lyric, let us briefly examine one of the few romances which adapted the epic mode and retained much of its feeling. This is the French romance *Perlesvaus*, which tells of Perlesvaus (Perceval) and his quest for the Holy Grail. In all the other versions of Perceval's story, he is in love with or married to Blancheflor, and there is therefore a substantial element of courtly love. *Perlesvaus*, however, is purely concerned with the struggle of Arthur and his knights to impose – by force if necessary – the New Law of Christianity in place of the evils of the Old Law. It is one of the strangest and most powerful of the romances, opening with a vivid picture of Arthur's court in decline because the King refuses to give the order for his knights to assemble and continuing through a series of magical adventures to Perceval's conquest of the Grail castle, the highest and most weighty of these enchantments. The mood of the romance is of the Christian knights as solitary adventurers in a hostile world; even when they triumph, as Lancelot does in the heathen islands towards the end of the book, their victory is fragile. Despite Perceval's achievement of the Grail, the romance continues with adventures in which the champions of the New Law are by no means always victorious, and ends with the disappearance of Perceval and the Grail from human ken.

Although there is nothing to suggest such a link, the closest historical parallel to the atmosphere of *Perlesvaus* is found in the wars against the pagans of Eastern Europe, which culminated, at about the time that *Perlesvaus* was written, in the formation of the Teutonic Order with the specific object of converting the heathen by conquest. There is a fervour about the knights' battles for the New Law which the later Grail romances never quite achieve, partly because they are integrated into the great cycle of romances which centre on Arthur rather than on the Grail, and hence the love of Lancelot and Guinevere and the earthly vanities of court life are always in the background. Something of this exaltation comes across in the passage describing the restoration of the Grail castle after Perceval's victory.

This high story tells us that when the castle had been conquered the Saviour of the world rejoiced and was greatly pleased. The Holy Grail reappeared in the chapel, and so did the lance with the bleeding head and the sword with which Saint John was beheaded, which Sir Gawain had won, and all the other relics, too, of which there were a great number, because God loved that place dearly. The hermits returned to their hermitages in the forests and served Our Lord as they had always done. Joseus stayed at the castle with Perceval as long as he wished, but the Good Knight went out once more to scour the land where the New Law was being neglected. He killed all those ,who would not believe in it, and the country was ruled and protected by him, and the Law of Our Lord exalted by his strength and valour. The priests and knights of his uncle, who had now returned to the castle, loved Perceval dearly, for they never saw his goodness fail; rather did his valour and his faith in God grow and intensify. They showed him his uncle's sepulchre before the altar in the chapel; the tomb was rich indeed, laden with precious stones, and the priests and knights testified that after the body had been laid in the tomb and they had departed, they came back and found the splendid sepulchre that could now be seen; they did not know how it could have been put there, save by Our Lord's command. And they said that every night there was a brilliant light as of candles, but they did not know where it came from unless it were from God.

The *Perlesvaus* is the most extreme of the Grail romances, which form an exceptional group in their strongly religious tendency. The mainstream of chivalric literature is determinedly secular, often amoral or immoral, and its morality or lack of it comes from very different sources, primarily the great flowering of lyric poetry in southern France in the troubadour period. The troubadours, whose surviving work dates from the twelfth to the fourteenth centuries, came from a rich, leisured society, which had time to develop a highly elaborate secular culture, something which the long centuries of warfare since the end of the Roman peace had discouraged elsewhere. They drew on the great lyrical love themes common to many cultures, just as the writers of the *chansons de geste* drew on the common stock of heroic themes and attitudes; but whereas the *chansons de geste* remained simple and direct, the troubadours produced poetry of astonishing sophistication. Even the earliest surviving poems, those of Guillaume IX, Duke of Aquitaine (grand-father of Eleanor of Aquitaine), suggest that the poets of the early twelfth century worked in a very polished style, because he parodies an already complex attitude to love in some of his songs. The centre, the pivot and lodestone of the troubadour's world is the lady whom he loves. Earlier lyrics appear to be almost equally divided between male and female lovers; the troubadours are almost exclusively concerned with the man's desire for an often distant and unattainable mistress. This is not to say that the troubadours wrote nothing but love poetry; there are many varieties of poems on topics ranging from the bawdy to the satirical, from the autobiographical to the religious, besides their love poetry, but it is the latter which had the greatest effect outside their own world.

In troubadour poetry there is a continual tension between the physical side of love, love shared and enjoyed, and the longing of an unfulfilled love. One troubadour will praise consummated love as the only true pleasure, while another will attack it as a passing sensation, not to be compared with the exquisite pleasure-pain of a love which is either impossible to fulfil or is deliberately denied fulfilment. But whatever the attitude to 'the right true end of love', love is regarded as the dominant force in a man's life. In order to win his lady, he has to gain favour in her eyes; so from his love stem all virtues of this world – valour, courtesy, generosity – summed up in the one word *pretz*, worth. The man who does not love can never hope to be as accomplished as the lover whose desire spurs him on to new achievements.

Guillaume of Aquitaine celebrates both physical and spiritual love with equal skill, but later poets tended more towards the spiritual side of love. Marcabru, writing twenty years later from 1130 to 1150, began to develop this theme. He is the 'most inventive and original of all the troubadours', and his poetry may reflect his personal circumstances. Guillaume was a great lord who could afford to keep noble mistresses; Marcabru was of humble or illegitimate birth and could not hope to compete in the world of physical love, where a fine appearance and a long purse counted for more than skill in poetry. He distinguishes in his poems between *Amars*, mere carnal love, and *fin' amors*, spiritual love. *Amars*, which he describes in the bluntest terms, is insatiable lust, which gives no satisfaction; *fin' amors* offers not only enduring pleasure but is a way through which man may discover his own nobler nature. That such a theme should have become popular means that it must have corresponded to real aspirations in the society in which Marcabru lived; and there is much to support this view.

The second quarter of the twelfth century marked a change of direction in the culture of southern France away from violence and warfare – the world of the *chansons de geste* – to a peaceful and prosperous world where the castle became the court, presided over by the lady as much as the lord. The so-called 'courts of love', where witty, beautiful and learned ladies sat in judgement on their errant lovers, have long since been shown to be a literary and romantic fiction; yet the image contains a grain of truth. Marriages were usually a matter of entirely unromantic feudal business, like the match between Geoffrey of Anjou and Matilda of England in 1127, when the bridegroom was fourteen and the bride twenty-five, and the couple were notoriously incompatible into the bargain; but from the match came the creation of the great Angevin empire which dominated twelfth-century France. However, once the lady was married, she acquired a status and authority not unlike that of her lord, particularly in the south, where Roman law, more favourable to women, was still current. The troubadour ethos of *fin' amors* would seem to offer spiritual fulfilment of just the kind to meet the situation: it is a kind of adulation, a tribute to grace and beauty in a world where physical love was chiefly concerned with the getting of heirs to estates;

Marcabru shows us a man 'doing a good day's work at night' by siring a fine
son through whom he will lord it over everyone.

Marcabru himself, however, is too fierce a moralist to write pure love-
poetry; his poems seem to define his moral ideal of *fin' amors* by what it is not,
just as a popular preacher might find better material in denouncing sins rather
than praising virtues. One of his greatest poems begins by such a contrast
between vice and virtue. 'The man who is the chosen one of *fin' amors* lives
happy, courtly and wise, and the one whom it rejects, it destroys...' He goes on
to prophesy a dire fate for those who stray from the true path:

> *Such are false judges, such are robbers,*
> *adulterous husbands, perjurers,*
> *false-painted men and slanderers,*
> *demagogues, cloister-pillagers,*
> *and those fervid courtesans*
> *who yield to other women's husbands –*
> *all these will have hellish reward!*
> *Drunken men and blackmailers,*
> *false clergy and false abbots too,*
> *false anchoresses, anchorites,*
> *will suffer there, says Marcabru:*
> *the false all have their place reserved –*
> *gracious Love has promised it –*
> *their grief there will be desperate!*

His list of sinners is taken from St Paul's *Epistle to the Galatians* – that
tremendous catalogue of errors that Browning remembered in another
context:

> *There's a great text in Galatians*
> *Once you trip on it, entails*
> *Twenty-nine distinct damnations,*
> *One sure, if another fails.*

As if to emphasise the way in which *fin' amors* is a parallel to Christianity
– almost a rival, for this is Provence, soon to harbour the Cathar heresy –
Marcabru returns to the positive view of love with a stanza which echoes St

Augustine and St John (the 'fountain of good' and 'the true light which lighteth the world'):

> *Ah, gracious Love, fountain of good,*
> *illuminating the whole world,*
> *I ask forgiveness for these cries –*
> *shield me from having to linger there!*
> *I hold myself your prisoner*
> *to have your comfort everywhere,*
> *hoping that you will be my guide.*

Elsewhere Marcabru outlines the ethics of this new religion, showing how *mesura*, restraint or moderation, is essential if a man is to achieve *cortesia*, the fullness of courtly virtues and actions. Both *mesura* and *cortesia* can be attained only through love.

With such a creed, set out in the most powerful rhetorical and emotional language, and not afraid to borrow from the highest images ,emotional religion, it is hardly surprising that troubadour poetry aroused its followers to scale new poetic heights. The love songs that Marcabru was temperamentally unable to write came from other, gentler hands. Later generations misunderstood these subtle poems and wove fairy tales around them: Bernart de Ventadorn, like Marcabru of humble birth, addressing a lyric to Eleanor of Aquitaine, was represented as her lover, while Jaufré Rudel, who proclaimed the merits of ideal, distant love, was the hero of a folktale in which he worshipped the unseen Countess of Tripoli in his poems, went to Palestine to seek the object of his sweet songs, only to die in her arms the moment he saw her. Jaufré Rudel's poetry in fact supplies what is missing in that of Marcabru, the love song based on *fin' amors*. His most famous lyric begins with a description of his longing:

> *When the days grow long in May*
> *I love to hear the distant bird;*
> *When I have left off listening*
> *It reminds me of my distant love*
> *And I go dull and bent with longing*
> *So that song, flower and hawthorn*
> *Might as well be winter frosts for me.*

He goes on to imagine that he does actually achieve his wish and is able to see and speak to his distant lady, to reach whom he will have to make a journey as long as a pilgrimage or crusade. But what will give him real joy is not so much the actual moment in her presence as the 'emotion recollected in tranquillity' afterwards.

Bernart de Ventadorn is the 'archetype of the courtly troubadour', and his work represents the full development of the troubadour ethic in the form in which it was to pass into the literature of chivalry proper. Ventadorn introduces one striking idea which at once linked the poetic world of the troubadours with the practical world of the knight: he sees himself as bound in service to his lady, just as the knight was bound in service to his lord. At once the evocative and familiar vocabulary of the feudal world is at his disposal; the often esoteric ideas are conveyed in a way which any knight can understand. The knight's training, too, is paralleled by that of the lover, who begins as a mere hopeful, and works his way, first as suppliant, then as accepted suitor, to the rarely achieved status of acknowledged lover. Bernart offers a convention, a formal structure of love, in place of the vague and elusive poetic idealism of his predecessors.

This new approach would have found little favour, however, if its proposer had not also been a great poet. The sophisticated simplicity of his poems does not come across easily in translation but a few lines of his *Non es maravelha* will convey something of the quality of his courtliness and strength of feeling:

> *Do not wonder if my verses*
> *Outstrip those of other poets,*
> *My heart is more afire with love*
> *And I am swift to do love's bidding.*

He goes on to praise love, and to describe the torment and joy of his own slavery to it, offering his submission to his lady:

> *Noble lady, I ask of you*
> *To take me as your servitor;*
> *I'll serve you as I would my lord,*
> *Whatever my reward shall be.*
> *Look, I am here at your command,*
> *You who are noble, gay and kind.*
> *You are no bear or lion's whelp*
> *Who'll kill me if I yield to you.*

Bernart's hoped-for reward was a lover's reward, whether physical or spiritual; but in the later development of the idea of love-service a new variation arises. Just as the origins of the feudal contract lay in an agreement between the vassal who served and the lord who rewarded and protected, so the lady appears as the knight's protector in tournament or battle. Her favour is all-important to his success; and the favour became a physical token, perhaps a sleeve or kerchief, worn on the knight's armour. In its highest development, the idea of prowess stemming from love went even further: just as the lover in troubadour poetry had won *pretz* and *cortesia* through love, so in a less sophisticated world the knight won physical strength from his love, and the thought of his beloved lent strength to his sword-arm. Malory describes how Sir Palomides, Tristram's rival for the love of Iseult, is inspired by the sight of her during a tournament:

> So when Iseult espied Sir Tristram again upon his horse's back, she was passing glad and then she laughed and was cheerful. And as it happened, Sir Palomides looked up towards her; she was in the window, and Sir Palomides espied how she laughed. And at that he took such joy that he smote down, either with his spear or with his sword, all the knights he met, for through the sight of her he was so enamoured in her love that it seemed as though if both Sir Tristram and Sir Lancelot had been against him, they would have won no honour from him.

This inspired strength was, of course, at the lady's command. In the romance of *Perlesvaus*, Gawain is made by a lady 'to perform worse than anyone at the tournament today, and to do all the cowardly deeds that a knight can do, and bear none but your own arms so that you may be more clearly recognized.' Gawain agrees, and carries out her commands to perfection:

> Another knight wanted to joust with Sir Gawain, but he avoided him and fled as fast as he could, pretending that he did not dare face an attack from anyone. He rode back to King Arthur for protection, and the King was deeply ashamed by what he had seen him do, and had to forget about fighting well that day. And he had great difficulty in defending and protecting Sir Gawain, for he was clinging as close to him as a magpie to a bush when falcons are trying to seize it. In this disgrace Sir Gawain remained throughout the tournament, and the knights all said that he had a far greater reputation than he deserved, for they had never seen so cowardly a knight at any tourney ...

But before we move into the world of the romances proper, we have still to look at two other important areas that contributed to the final shape of chivalric literature. The Provençal poets were not alone in their evolution of a complex love poetry; in Germany, too, the ideal of love was celebrated by poets who carried the title of 'love-singers', *minnesänger*. Although the later and better-known *minnesänger* borrowed their verse-forms, and often the tunes to which their poems were sung, from Provence, for their imagery and ideas they drew on a flourishing native poetic tradition of which only fragments have come down to us. The *minnesänger* are much more forthright in their attitudes to love, and while acknowledging the high ideals, are equally ready to mock those who carry them to excess. The earliest of the German poets, Der von Kürenberc, is a contemporary of Bernart de Ventadorn: he has obviously heard a good deal about idealised love, and is prepared to satirise a lover who is such an idealist that he has no time for physical love:

> *'Late last night I stood   before your bed,*
> *and I did not dare   to wake you, lady.'*
> *'May God hate you for this for ever!*
> *After all, I wasn't a wild boar,'   the lady said.*

The German poets are also well aware of the lady's point of view. In the troubadours' poems, the lady very rarely has anything to say; ideals and visions are all the more impressive if they stay silent, and the troubadours' world depended on raising the lady to almost mystical heights. Kürenberc, on the other hand, is quite prepared to put the point of view of a lady abandoned by her lover, and to put it most eloquently:

> *I trained myself a falcon through a year's long days.*
> *When he was safely tamed to follow my ways*
> *And his plumage shone golden, painted by my hand,*
> *With powerful wingbeats rising, he sought another land.*
>
> *Since then I've often seen him soaring in fair flight,*
> *For on his feet my silken jesses still shine bright*
> *And his plumage gleams with scarlet and with gold.*
> *May God grace lovers and reunite them as of old.*

Minnesang, as a result, is a much broader tradition, ranging from great poets such as Walther von der Vogelweide, who have a timeless freedom from all conventions and can see beyond the formalities of courtly love, to the technical virtuosos who foreshadow the craft of the later '*meistersinger*', poets for whom elaborate form was all too often more important than poetic content. As an example of these contrasts, here is Walther von der Vogelweide playing on the words *frouwe*, lady, and *wip*, woman, and coming to an unexpected conclusion:

> *'Woman' will always be woman's highest name –*
> *it honours her more than 'lady', if I'm right.*
> *If any look on being a woman as shame,*
> *let her first heed my song, and then decide.*
> *Among ladies some are unwomanly,*
> *among women this cannot be.*
> *Woman's name and woman's being,*
> *they are both so lovable –*
> *whatever else ladies may be,*
> *let them at least be womanly!*
> *A doubtful praise can mean disdain*
> *– like the word 'lady' now and then –*
> *but the name 'woman' gives each one a crown.*

Walther is in effect saying: 'Your courtly conventions are all very well, but there are deeper human truths which are more important.'

But for Ulrich von Lichtenstein, poet and jouster, convention is everything. He it was who, to honour his lady, undertook a long journey through Italy, Austria and Bohemia in 1227, of which he left a romantic narrative in verse: he says that he went dressed as Frau Venus, in honour of his lady, and in one month's jousting broke 307 spears. His choice of combat is significant: the joust was much better adapted to the needs of a knight striving to honour his lady than the free-for-all of the tournament, because individual prowess was at stake. Ulrich's exploits are only fifty years after those of William Marshal; yet they are a world apart, in that William fights for his own gain, with comrades and friends. Ulrich fights alone, sustained not by comradeship but by his idealised love for his lady – who, alas, proved too harsh; when he next set out on a series of jousts, thirteen years later, it was in honour of a new lady. The lyric that follows demonstrates his *credo* of service and honour:

The Knight and Warfare

Throughout the medieval period, the knight's central preoccupation was with warfare, whether in the king's service, on crusade, or even in private warfare. Most of the spectacular armour that survives is from tournaments, but it gives a better idea of the equipment than the few remaining pieces of war armour, less decorative and more practical but rarely in good shape.

Major battles were infrequent, but could have immense consequences; few knights would actually experience such an occasion. Sieges were the major part of medieval warfare, often protracted and wearisome for the attackers as well as the defenders. The engineers and artillery might break down the city's walls, but in the final assault it was the knights who led the way.

Richard I, depicted on a tile from Chertsey Abbey

The crusades were for two centuries the focal point of much knightly activity, and for a time there were more dramatic events in military terms in the Near East than in the whole of western Europe. When the Holy Land was lost, the Knights Hospitallers withdrew to Rhodes, which they lost in the great siege of 1480, and then to Malta, which they successfully defended in 1525. The Templars, by contrast, were disbanded, and the leaders of the Order were burnt as heretics in 1313.

ARMOUR

Hilt of a sword said to be that of Edward III; the sword was always the knight's most treasured possession, and hilts were often elaborately decorated and could contain sacred relics

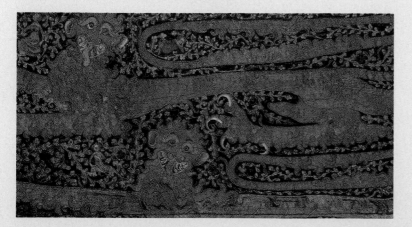

(above left) *A jousting helm of the thirteenth century; the helm itself is very similar to the helm for war, but the crest would only be used in the lists*

(above right) *Flemish parade shield for the jousts, showing a scene of courtly love*

(left) *An embroidered horse banner with the arms of Edward III*

THE CRUSADERS

(right) *The burning of Jacques de Molay, Master of the Templars, and two other leaders of the Order at Paris, 1313*

(below) The Siege of Malta, Assault on the Castilian Knights, August 1565 *by Aleccis Malteo Perez*

(opposite top) *Moslems defending Antioch against the crusaders in 1099*

(opposite below left) *The attack on Damietta during St Louis' expedition to Egypt, 1260*

(opposite below right) *Preparations for the defence of Rhodes, 1480*

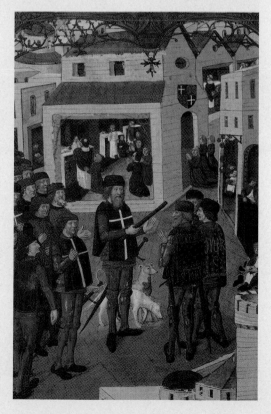

BATTLES & SIEGES

The battle of Crécy: a spectacular English victory about which chivalric legends grew up

(top left) *Knights with prisoners and cattle captured on a raid: this economic warfare was a major part of campaigns in the Hundred Years' War*

(left) *Knights at a besieged city: this was the most arduous and wearying type of warfare*

BATTLES & SIEGES

Siege engines: a trebuchet with winch and sling

Knights who seek for honour, you should make sure
Of serving when you're armed ladies of worth
If you wish to use your time
In knight's ways, with honour,
Pay court to fairest women.

Your courage should be high as you bear shield
You should be polished, bold, blithe and gentle
Serve knighthood with all your skill
And be glad, set love high,
Thus you shall win high praises.

Think now of the greetings of great ladies,
How sweet they make the life of their dear friends.
He who wins ladies' greetings
Wins honour, his desire;
His joy is all the sweeter.

The knight who with his shield will ward off shame
Should always strive to use his utmost strength
For deeds of arms bring honour.
Worth and praise are his due,
But both are dearly purchased.

A man's heart is tested in deeds of arms
Cowardice is always foreign to arms
False is that man to woman
Who has fear in the heart
Which he covers with his shield!

Bring my shield here! Today you shall see me
In the service of my dearest lady.
I must win her to my love;
She shall greet me or I
Perish as I strive to serve.

By my toil and service I will bring her
To love me more than I love her myself
Many spears shall break on me.
Now fetch me spear and sword!
That will make her smile on me;
That will make her kind to me!

Like the troubadours, the heyday of the *minnesänger* was relatively brief; the anarchy of Germany after Frederick II's death in 1250 brought the world of courtly culture on which they depended to an end, just as the Albigensian Crusade had ended the full flowering of Provençal culture. Their poetry, wider-ranging in its themes, leads directly into later German poetry, while Provençal poetry died out in the succeeding century; its legacy was inherited by the first Italian poets and leads out of the world of chivalry into the humanist world of Dante.

The most surprising source of the material of the chivalric romances takes us far from Dante's Italy. It is the ancient literature of the Celtic world, which was mostly preserved in oral form, to be recited by highly trained poets. The Celtic 'romances' are a mixture of ancient myths about the Celtic, gods, of folklore, and of history. But what particularly appealed to the French poets and their knightly audiences was that element of the marvellous, the irrational and

This fourteenth century ivory mirror case from Paris shows an allegorical siege, where knights besiege the castle of love, which is defended by ladies

supernatural, which pervades the stories. We can only guess at the ways in which Celtic romance came to the attention of French poets. It may be that the contact was through Brittany, but very little authentic Breton tradition survives against which to test this theory.

A more probable area, where French-speaking knights and their followers were in close contact with a Celtic people, is South Wales in the late eleventh and early twelfth centuries. Geoffrey of Monmouth, writing his fictional history of Britain in the 1130s, which is the first surviving book to give us the story of King Arthur, certainly drew on Welsh tradition, and it seems likely that most of the Celtic material to be found in French poems came from Welsh sources. Again, the difficulty is that the surviving Welsh romances were written down later than the first French romances, and some of them show distinct traces of courtly and chivalric ideas. However, eight of the eleven stories known to English readers as *The Mabinogion* reflect a world untouched by such themes. One episode will have to suffice to give some idea of its flavour. Pryderi and Manawydan are out hunting one day when their hounds pursue a 'shining white' wild boar into a newly-built caer or fortress which neither of the hunters had ever seen before. Both hounds and quarry vanish, and despite Manawydan's warning Pryderi goes into the caer:

When he came to the caer neither man nor beast nor the boar nor the dogs nor house nor habitation could he see in the caer. As it were in the middle of the caer floor, he could see a fountain with marble work around it, and on the edge of the fountain a golden bowl fastened to four chains, and that upon a marble slab, and the chains ascending into the air, and he could see no end to them. He was transported with the great beauty of the gold and with the exceeding good workmanship of the bowl, and he came to where the bowl was and laid hold of it. And as soon as he laid hold of the bowl, his two hands stuck to the bowl, and his feet to the slab on which he was standing, and all his power of speech forsook him, so that he could not utter one word. And thus he stood.

And Manawydan waited for him till near the close of day. And late in the afternoon, when he was convinced he would get no tidings of Pryderi or of the dogs, he came to the court. As he came inside, Rhiannon looked on him. 'Where,' said she, 'are thy companion and thy dogs?' 'Here,' he replied, 'is my story.' And he told it all. 'Faith,' said Rhiannon, 'a bad comrade hast thou been, but a good comrade hast thou lost.' And with that word out she went, and in the direction he told her the man and the caer were, thither she proceeded. She saw the gate of the caer open; there was no concealment on it, and in she came. And as soon as she came, she perceived Pryderi laying hold of the bowl, and she came towards him. 'Alas, my lord,' said she, 'what dost thou here?' And she laid hold of the bowl with him, and as soon as she laid hold, her own hands stuck to the bowl and her feet to the slab, so that she too was not able to utter one word. And with that, as soon as it was night, lo, a peal of thunder over them, and a fall of mist, and thereupon the caer vanished, and, away with them too.

The story reveals that this magic is part of an enchantment placed on Pryderi's lands in revenge for a trick that had been played years before on a kinsman of the magician.

When the French writers took over these stories, or episodes, they retained the *matière* or actual events, but radically altered the *sen*, or wider context and meaning. Instead of the closed Celtic world of warring princelings, where kinship and revenge were all-important, they transformed the marvels into a kind of test of valour for knights; their heroes could distinguish themselves by overcoming these terrors by their own heroic qualities, their *pretz* and *cortesia*, and this in turn stemmed from their chosen lady. So on to this supernatural world was grafted a logic which overcame it; chivalry was the dominant theme, the supernatural a secondary consideration – but one which the poet's listeners undoubtedly relished.

The surviving Welsh stories are fragmentary; we have no complete cycle of stories, but rather episodes from longer works. The French romance writers inherited this liking for a wider theme, partly because it enabled poets to lure patrons or audiences by promising another story in the same vein, and many romances survive with a note at the end indicating that there is a continuation. In some cases, such a note may well have been a hint to the patron to commission the next instalment rather than evidence of its existence.

The links between one romance and another did not have to be substantial, and so three supposedly historical figures became the focal points for the romances. The first was Charlemagne, who already played a large part in the *chansons de geste*, often because the kernel of historical fact around which the legends had grown up was in fact drawn from his reign or that of his sons. The second was Alexander the Great, because the earliest romances proper had had Greek themes. The later Latin literature, preserved in monasteries since the end of the Roman Empire in the West, included a large amount of secular literature, and it was from the partly romanticised versions of the Greek heroic stories as retold by fourth-century poets that the first French romances were drawn. The earliest surviving fragments are from a version of the story of Alexander written in south-east France in the early twelfth century. In the mid-twelfth century versions of the *Aeneid*, the *Iliad* and the story of Oedipus were produced: Benoit de Ste Maure, who reworked the *Iliad*, introduced a love-story into his otherwise heroic material and so gave us Troilus and Cressida, whose history was to be retold by many later medieval poets. This change was typical of the reworking of the classical stories: the Greek heroes appear as knights or courtly lovers. But the absence of miracles and high adventure meant that the relatively restrained *Aeneid* and *Iliad* material was abandoned in favour of the stories about Alexander, to whom all kinds of Oriental folklore and tales about the riches of the East were attached, to supply the *frisson* offered in a different context by the Celtic supernatural.

The third and most familiar figure at the centre of the romances is that of King Arthur, and it is from the tales concerning him that we shall draw our examples of fully developed chivalric romance. Arthur himself is often a shadowy figure, and his own story is only slightly elaborated between Geoffrey of Monmouth's version in the twelfth century and, Sir Thomas Malory's in the fifteenth. Yet he acted as a magnet for a vast range of stories which originally had nothing to do with him, because his court became an archetype of all knightly courts. For one thing, Arthur himself was a Celtic figure, and it is the romances centred on him that contain almost all the Celtic magic and mysteries taken over by French poets. It is accepted that great quests and adventures are a commonplace at Arthur's court: take the opening of the independent romance of 'The Fair Unknown' – the unknown youth who appears at court, is driven away but proves to be a hero – which appears in Malory as 'The Tale of Sir Gareth of Orkney':

> In Arthur's days, when he held the Round Table in full splendour, it came about that the King commanded that the high feast of Pentecost should be held at a city and castle, that was called Kynke Kenadonne in those days, on the seashore on the borders of Wales. And the King always had a custom that at the feast of Pentecost in particular, above any other feast in the year, he would never sit down to eat until he had heard or seen some great marvel. And because of that custom all kinds of strange adventures came before Arthur, particularly on that feastday.

The ease with which other tales can be added means that it is only in the Arthurian cycle that the four strands we identified at the beginning of the chapter can merge fully: Arthur's own story provides the epic element, the casting of the material is in the romance form, the adventures are drawn from the Celtic marvels, and the conduct of the central characters is determined by the code of courtly love. However, the forging of these elements into a single cycle was a gradual one, and the great strength of the stories about Arthur was – and still is – that they are diverse enough to be adapted to changing tastes.

The earliest fully-fledged Arthurian romances are those of Chrétien de Troyes, who introduces us for the first time to two of their central characters – Lancelot and Perceval – as well as being the first to integrate the Celtic marvels into the romance form. His early romance, *Le Chevalier au Lion*, opens with a splendid example of this. It is a warm Whitsun afternoon at Arthur's court; the King has fallen asleep, and the knights are whiling away the time by talking about their exploits. Calogrenant is persuaded by the Queen to speak about an old adventure of his, which did not turn out entirely to his credit and about which he had therefore kept silent. Seven years before, he said, he had been 'making his way in search of adventures, fully armed as a knight should be':

That night I was made welcome as a guest, and my horse was ready as soon as it was daybreak, just as I had requested the night before. My good host and his dear daughter I commended to the Holy Ghost and said farewell at once, leaving as soon as I could. I had scarcely left the castle when I came to a clearing where wild bulls were fighting amongst themselves, making such a noise and looking so fierce, that, to tell the truth, I beat a retreat; for there is no animal as fierce and dangerous as a bull. I saw a peasant, black as a mulberry, extremely huge and hideous, – indeed, I cannot describe how ugly he was – sitting on a stump. with a great club in his hand. I approached him and saw that his head was bigger than a horse's; he had tousled hair, but he was bald in front, with a forehead a foot high, and had great hairy ears like an elephant's. Huge eyebrows overhung his flat face, with its owl's eyes and cat's nose, a long wolf's mouth and sharp yellow teeth like a boar's. He had a black beard and tangled moustache, and although he was tall his body was twisted. He leaned on his club, dressed in a strange garment, not made of linen or cotton, but of two newly-flayed hides from bulls or oxen, fastened round his neck. As soon as he saw me approach, the peasant got up; I did not know if he was going to attack me, or what he was going to do, but I prepared to defend myself until I saw that when he stood up properly on a tree trunk, he was over seventeen feet tall. He looked at me without a word, just like a dumb animal, and I thought that he was an idiot and could not speak. Anyway, I plucked up courage and said to him: 'Go on, tell me if you are friend or enemy.' He answered: 'I am a man.' 'What kind of man?' 'Just as you see me, never different.' 'What do you do here?' 'I live here, keeping these cattle in the wood.' 'Keeping them? By St Peter of Rome, they would not obey a man, and anyway, how can you keep cattle in the open or in a wood without a place to shut them in?' 'I keep them in such a way that they never leave this clearing.' 'And you can make them obey? Tell me how do you do it.' 'None of them dares to move off

Episodes from the romance of Yvain, showing the adventures of a twelfth-century knight-errant

when they see me coming, because when I get one into my hard strong hands I give its horns such a twisting that the others tremble with fear, and gather round me as if to beg for mercy. Only I can come here, because anyone else would be killed by them at once. So I am lord of my cattle; and now it is your turn to tell me who you are and what you seek.' 'I am a knight, and I seek something I cannot find; indeed I have sought it for a long time and still cannot find it.' 'And what are you after?' 'Adventures to prove my courage and boldness, so please tell me if you know of any adventure or marvel.' 'You will have to do without "adventures" because I know nothing about such things, and have never heard of them. But if you go to a fountain near here, you won't come back without difficulty, if you follow the custom. Near here there is a path which leads straight to it, but make sure that you follow the straight path because there are many other paths on which to lose your way. There you will see a fountain of boiling water which is colder than marble. It is shaded by the finest tree that Nature ever made. Its leaves last for ever, it does not lose them in winter; from it hangs an iron bowl on a chain so long that it reaches the fountain. By the fountain there is a great stone – you will see it, but I can't describe it, because I've never seen one like it – and on the other side a chapel, which is small but very beautiful. If you scoop up some water in the bowl and pour it on the stone, you will see such a storm that no wild animal will stay in the forest; every dog, stag, deer and boar and all the birds will leave it in terror, because you will see such lightning, wind and shattering of trees, rain and thunder, that if you get away unharmed you will be luckier than any of the knights who have been there before.'

So I left the peasant who had shown me the way. It must have been after nine, and getting on towards noon when I saw the tree and the chapel. The tree was the finest pine tree that ever grew on the earth; however hard it rained, not a drop of water would have penetrated its branches. I saw the bowl hanging from the tree, made of finer gold than you can buy at any fair, and believe me, the fountain was boiling like hot water. The stone was an emerald, with a hole in it like a flask, set with four rubies, brighter and more brilliant red than the sun when it rises in the East. And every word of what follows is true. I wanted to see the marvellous. storm and tempest, which was not a wise thing to do, for I would have been glad to stop it, if I could have done so, as soon as I had poured water from the bowl on to the stone. I must have poured too much, for the sky was so stormy that lightning struck from more than fourteen directions at once. The storm was so violent that a hundred times I expected to be killed by the thunderbolts and shattered trees that fell all around me, and I was terrified as long as the storm lasted. But God comforted me, because the tempest did not last long, and the winds, which obey His commands, died down. I was delighted to see the air become clear and pure, and my joy made me forget my fear. As soon as the storm passed, I saw gathered on the great pine tree so many birds that every branch and leaf was covered with them, making the tree even more beautiful; they all began to sing, and although they were in perfect harmony, none of them sang the same song. Their joyful song was a delight, and I listened to them until they had finished their 'service'; I do not think that anyone else will find such pleasure in singing unless he hears those same birds, which almost sent me out of my mind with ecstasy.

Then I heard a knight approaching: indeed I thought there were ten knights, he made such a noise. When I saw that he was alone, I held my horse and mounted at once. He rode towards me angrily, faster than a swallow and fiercer than a lion, challenging me in a loud voice: 'Vassal, you never challenged me but have done me much harm just the same. If you have a quarrel with me, you should have challenged me, but now I demand satisfaction as you have declared war on me. If I can I shall take revenge for the damage which you can see you have done: look at my woods, which you have destroyed. I accuse you of driving me from my house by storms and rain. You have caused me harm, such harm to my woods and castle, that no men-at-arms nor walls could have protected me; no one would have been safe even in a stone fortress. So there can never be any truce or peace between us.'

The 'adventure' recalls that of Pryderi in the *Mabinogion*, but the emphasis is subtly altered. Calogrenant actively *seeks* adventures, while Pryderi's one wish is to hold his lands in peace. The outcome of the telling of his story is that his cousin Yvain goes to the spring, kills the knight who defends it, and, by marrying his widow Laudine, becomes the new defender of the spring. But the romance does not end there, for Yvain's wooing of his new bride, albeit carried out with much heartsearching and play on the ways of love, has been brief: he has had none of the trials of love. So Chrétien has his hero lured away by Gawain to new deeds of arms, promising Laudinc to return within a year. The promise is forgotten, and Yvain is reproached by his lady, at which he goes mad, and his adventures begin again. The penance is long and hard and of course involves many more adventures; in the course of them he is cured of his madness, rescues a lion which becomes his faithful companion, and rescues several ladies from injustice. Finally, he returns to the magic spring as challenger, and Laudine, bereft of a champion to defend her lands, at last pardons him and accepts him back. So the mysterious adventure becomes the key to a psychological romance, satisfying in both its richness of plot and skilful handling of motive and character: in short, Chrétien succeeds in appealing to knight and lady alike, the essential requirement for chivalric literature. Furthermore, Calogrenant's recital of the central adventure, as John Stevens points out in his *Medieval Romance*, is a subtle use of a 'marvel' to convey philosophical ideas: the giant is the type of man as mere rational animal, while Calogrenant, the knight, is man in his true guise as spiritual seeker. 'Adventures' are beyond the ken of men who are merely content to exist: "the aspiring mind' belonged to the medieval knight before it belonged to the Renaissance hero.'

Chrétien's romances were to set the pattern for most of the later works in this vein; many episodes in Malory's great summing-up of the Arthurian stories at the end of the Middle Ages are to be found in Chrétien three centuries earlier. However, his material included not only 'adventures' from the Welsh or Breton sources, but also fully fledged heroes with recognised characteristics. It is perhaps through the heroes that we can best trace the development of the romances.

The first major Arthurian hero is Gawain, Arthur's nephew, in Geoffrey of Monmouth. Chrétien gives him an important part to play in three of his romances, but his character is already fixed, and he is at times slightly out of place in the author's world. He is one of the greatest and most skilful knights alive, courtly and polished, but he has no great respect for love-service, preferring casual physical encounters to the spiritual ideals, of courtly love. The stories about him are distantly derived from those about the Irish hero Cuchulainn, and frequently involve magic.

The most famous of the romances about him, *Sir Gawain and the Green Knight*, is centred on the so-called 'beheading game' in which a mysterious challenger dares any knight to cut off his head if he will face a return blow in a year's time. When the challenge is accepted and carried out, the stranger picks up his head and disappears after reminding Gawain of the second part of the bargain. When Gawain comes to the stranger's castle, the outcome of the return blow is made to depend on Gawain's success in resisting the temptation offered by the stranger's beautiful wife. For three days the stranger goes hunting while Gawain is entertained by the lady, and at the end of each day they exchange spoils. On the last day, however, Gawain accepts a magic girdle from the lady, which will protect him from any deadly blow, and does not give it to his host. For this, when Gawain faces his ordeal, the host gives him two feint blows, and the third time grazes his neck. The poet has transformed the original tales into a subtle masterpiece; but even here echoes of the old image of Gawain persist, a hero equal to shape-shifters and magicians, and proud of his sexual prowess: the taking of the girdle replaces possession of the lady herself.

Even in the courtly world of Chrétien's romances, Gawain's adventures often include scenes which must have represented the wishful thinking of many a knight, as beautiful girls who have only set eyes on him hours before come naked to his bedside at midnight. Sometimes there are complications, as in the adventure of the magic bed, where a sword descends and attacks Gawain

Gawain, one of the first Arthurian heroes, jousts with Girofles

each time he moves towards the girl lying beside him, but even this obstacle forces him into chastity for only one night; their love is consummated the following evening. Gawain remains the old-fashioned hero to the end; even in the closing pages of Malory, in his great duel with Lancelot, his strength magically increases threefold with the sun, reaching its height at midday, and waning thereafter. Because he conforms to the courtly ideal in prowess alone, and flouts the accepted code of love, Gawain is presented in the later romances as a kind of flawed hero, a valiant but earthbound character, more suited to the world of epic myths in which he originated.

By contrast, Tristan (Tristram, as he was known in the later romances) is less of a knight than a lover in the first stories about him. The earliest recorded version is an Anglo-Norman poem, now lost, of about 1150. The crux of the story is a simple one: Tristan, sent to fetch his king's bride, Iseult, from Ireland, drinks a love-potion with her as they return together to Cornwall. The story of passion and treachery that follows derives entirely from this single act, and Tristan and Iseult stand for the archetype of all-consuming star-crossed love. The earliest versions seem to have been little more than a love-story, such as might be found in almost any literature, but the tale was too close to the ideals of courtly love to go unnoticed by the troubadours and their followers. Tristan is practically the only romance hero to be mentioned in a troubadour poem, and his story was recast in courtly fashion by the poet Thomas in about 1160. There is good reason to think that Thomas' poem was written for Eleanor of Aquitaine and her circle, and indeed it is more concerned with the ethics of love than of chivalry. And yet neither Thomas nor the poets who took up the

Gawain fights ten footsoldiers: the mounted knight always saw himself as superior to infantry

story in succeeding centuries ever reconciled Tristan and Iseult's love with the ideals of courtly love. Courtly love has a strongly moral streak in it, a kind of secular morality replacing that of the Church: the lover must keep faith, he must strive towards the grail of his lady's affections through prowess and self-improvement. None of this appears in Tristan's story. He wins his lady through an entirely chance event, and she surrenders at once and totally to him. Their subsequent adventures are dictated by their passion, love which overwhelms all morality and yet has to be reconciled in practical terms with everyday life.

Tiles depicting the story of Tristan and Iseult: Tristan brings Iseult to Cornwall and Tristan harping to Mark

When Gottfried von Strassburg came to write his version of the story in the early thirteenth century, he depicts Tristan struggling with loyalty and honour before he succumbs to the effect of the potion: and it is clear that loyalty and honour are part of the everyday world and not of the world of love. The otherness of this love-world is underlined by one of the central episodes, Tristan and Iseult's escape from the mundane in the Cave of Lovers. Gottfried's picture of their life there underlines how little need of the courtly world his lovers have:

Nor were they greatly troubled that they should be alone in the wilds without company. Tell me, whom did they need in there with them, and why should anyone join them? They made an even number: there were simply one and one. Had they included a third in the even pair which they made, there would have been an uneven number, and they would have been much encumbered and embarrassed by the odd one. Their company of two was so ample a crowd for this pair that good King Arthur never held a feast in any of his palaces that gave keener pleasure or delight. In no land could you have found enjoyment for which these two would have given a brass farthing to have with them in their grotto. Whatever one

could imagine or conceive elsewhere in other countries to make a paradise, they had with them there. They would not have given a button for a better life, save only in respect of their honour. What more should they need? They had their court, they were amply supplied with all that goes to make for happiness. Their loyal servitors were the green lime, the sunshine and the shade, the brook and its banks, flowers, grass, blossoms, and leaves, so soothing to the eye. The service they received was the song of the birds, of the lovely, slender nightingale, the thrush and blackbird, and other birds of the forest. Siskin and calander-lark vied in eager rivalry to see who could give the best service. These followers served their ears and sense unendingly. Their high feast was Love, who gilded all their joys; she brought them King Arthur's Round Table as homage and all its company a thousand times a day! What better food could they have for body or soul? Man was there with Woman, Woman was there with Man. What else should they be needing? They had what they were meant to have, they had reached the goal of their desire.

Gottfried is too great an artist to be bound by any formal convention. He pays lip-service to the idea that love fosters moral virtues – 'Love is so blissful a thing, so blessed an endeavour, that apart from its teaching none attains worth or reputation' – but the actions of his characters betray him; Tristan and Iseult betray Mark again and again, and sacrifice even the faithful Brangane to their love. There is something elemental at work, which goes beyond ordinary bonds and allegiances.

So, in a sense, the story of Tristan and Iseult is almost the reverse of courtly and chivalric; and yet it was to form a major part of the Arthurian stories. The romance called the *Prose Tristan* was immensely popular, and is entirely orthodox in its presentation of the knightly world. For this to come about, Tristan and Iseult had to be brought down to the level of ordinary lovers: Tristan becomes another of the champions of the Round Table, a knight-errant and partaker in tournaments, Iseult another of the ladies watching from the lists. Only occasionally does the earlier story break through, when they leave court to live together in the forest; but their unconventional behaviour is doubly excused, first because they are bound by the love-potion, and second because King Mark, an ambivalent and potentially tragic figure in the early versions, is now portrayed as an out-and-out villain, capable of the worst behaviour.

Neither Tristan nor Gawain is a purely chivalric hero: there are traces of wider worlds in their characters. For the pure-bred, chivalric knight, we must look to Lancelot. Here we return to Chrétien de Troyes, but there is something strange about the author's relationship to his hero for, in the poem in which Lancelot first appears, *Le Chevalier de la charrette* (*The Knight of the Cart*), Chrétien insists that he wrote about Lancelot only because he was told to, and he left the poem to be finished by another hand. Perhaps it was that Lancelot was too perfect a lover, or perhaps Chrétien disliked the theme of adulterous love – though he claimed to have written a version of the Tristan story, now lost. Lancelot's story combines three separate themes: he is the best knight in the world, he serves the best lady in the world (but that lady is Arthur's Queen, Guinevere), and their love is consummated. He is Gawain, shorn of his magic powers, merged with Tristan and brought within the courtly convention.

Iseult tries to kill Tristan, because he had killed Morholt, who was betrothed to her

There is a feeling that his behaviour is dictated by a code of conduct rather than by instinct, and this is underlined by two episodes in the poem. The poem gets its title from the moment when Lancelot, hastening to rescue Guinevere from Meleagant who has abducted her, finds himself on foot; the only means of transport is a passing cart, such as hangmen use. He hesitates to bring shame on himself by letting it seem that he is being taken to execution; but the code that controls his honour comes into conflict with the code of love, and when he at last finds Guinevere, he is soundly rebuked for his hesitation: does he then not love her to the uttermost? If so, he should not have hesitated for a moment. Later, the same conflict is used to prove Lancelot's identity when he enters a tournament incognito:

> When Lancelot entered the tournament, he was as good as twenty of the best, and he began to fight so doughtily that no one could take his eyes from him, wherever he was. On the Pomelegloi side there was a brave and valorous knight, and his horse was spirited and swifter than a wild stag. He was the son of the Irish king, and fought well and handsomely. But the unknown knight pleased them all a hundred times more. In wonder they all make haste to ask: 'Who is this knight who fights so well?' And the Queen privily called a clever and wise damsel to her and said: 'Damsel, you must carry a message, and do it quickly and with few words. Go down from the stand, and approach yonder knight with the vermilion shield, and tell him privately that I bid him do his 'worst'.' She goes quickly, and with intelligence executes the Queen's command. She sought the knight until she came up close to him; then she said to him prudently and in a voice so low that no one standing by might hear: 'Sire, my lady the Queen sends you word by me that you shall do your 'worst'.' When he heard this, he replied: 'Very willingly,' like one who is altogether hers. Then he rides at another knight as hard as his horse can carry him, and misses his thrust which should have struck him. From that time till evening fell he continued to do as badly as possible in accordance with the Queen's desire. But the other, who fought with him, did not miss his thrust, but struck him with such violence that he was roughly handled. Thereupon he took to flight, and after that he never turned his horse's head toward any knight, and were he to die for it, he would never do anything unless he saw in it his shame, disgrace, and dishonour; he even pretends to be afraid of all the knights who pass to and fro. And the very knights who formerly esteemed him now hurled jests and jibes at him.

There are parallels for such behaviour in the rules formulated in Andreas the Chaplain's *On the Art of Love*, which also comes from the court of Marie de Champagne, for whom Chrétien wrote *Le Chevalier de la charrette*: Andreas uses phrases such as 'he who loves is very obedient', and 'love and courtesy consist in doing what one can for one's mistress'. But it was exactly this conventional world which corresponded most closely to the reality of courtly life. In broad terms, Lancelot's greatest feats are performed in tournaments, while Gawain has more to do with the marvellous happenings of knight-errantry; Lancelot's love, except for its consummation, is outwardly the harmless social amusement of love-service, while Tristan offers no such polite compliments to Iseult. Precisely because he represented an imaginable extension of real and everyday courtly life, Lancelot was to prove the most popular of the three heroes. *The Prose Lancelot* was the largest of all the Arthurian romances, and came to include almost the whole history of Arthur and his court: and in Malory, Lancelot is the knight without peer among sinful men. Sir Ector's lament for him sums up all the virtues of secular knighthood:

> Ah, Lancelot, thou wert head of all Christian knights! And now I dare say, thou Sir Lancelot, there thou liest, that thou wert never material of earthly knight's hand. And thou wert the most courteous knight that ever bore shield! And thou wert the truest friend to thy lover that ever bestrode horse, and thou wert the truest lover, of a sinful man, that ever loved woman, and thou wert the kindest man that ever struck with sword. And thou wert the goodliest person that ever came among press of knights, and thou wast the meekest man and the gentlest that ever ate in hall among ladies, and thou wert the sternest knight to thy mortal foe that ever put spear in the rest

Yet Lancelot is more than the sum of all the conventional chivalric virtues. His love for Guinevere, though it is expressed in a very different form, is closely related to that of Tristan and Iseult, and his story is clearly modelled on that of Tristan. Both are the best knights of the court; both love the king's wife; both eventually elope with her, Tristan to the forest, Lancelot to joyous Gard. Incidents in Lancelot's story are drawn directly from that of Tristan, such as the bloodstained bed when Lancelot makes love to the Queen when he is wounded. (The episode where he rescues Guinevere from the stake is taken from Yvain's rescue of Lunete in *Le Chevalier au lion*, and several of his lesser

The Reign
of Chivalry

(right) *Guinevere,
accused of adultery with
Lancelot, is led to the
stake; Lancelot rescues
her, but in so doing brings
about the downfall of the
Round Table*

(below) *The procession
of the Holy Grail, the
story which combines
spiritual ideals with those
of chivalry*

adventures originally belonged to Gawain.) It is, in fact, the very tension between Lancelot's love for Guinevere and his place in the conventional world that makes their history more than a pale shadow of Tristan's. Tristan and Iseult, absolved from responsibility by the *deus ex machina* of the love potion, owe no allegiances but to each other: their tragedy is personal. Lancelot and Guinevere, because they are so deeply enmeshed in the world of the court, bring ruin not merely to themselves but to Arthur, the Round Table and the whole kingdom.

Lancelot is always presented as the best knight in the world; and so he is, if by the world we mean secular life. But the romances were often written by men educated by the Church – clerics or clerks – who appear in medieval satires as the rivals of knights. We have already touched on the *Perlesvaus*, with its religious overtones; and it is only one of a group of Arthurian romances which replaced the worldly standards of courtly love with the higher calling of religion. Again, it is one of Chrétien's poems that is the starting point. His *Conte del graal* (*The Story of the Grail*) tells of the hero Perceval, brought up in secluded innocence by his mother, because she does not want him to share his father's fate, a knightly death on the battlefield. However, his noble nature leads him to seek knighthood, and his innocence qualifies him to solve the mysterious curse laid on the Fisher King, who is condemned to lie grievously wounded until a stranger should come to his castle, should watch the solemn ritual enacted there, and ask the vital question: 'Who is served by the Grail?' Perceval arrives at the castle, but as he has only been instructed in courtly ways, he represses his natural curiosity, remembering that it is not polite to ask too many questions. The next morning the castle is deserted, and Perceval later learns the effect of his failure to ask the question; but it is too late, and he cannot find his way back.

Chrétien never completed the poem, and never really explained what he meant by the Grail, but it seems that he was drawing on Christian tradition, and on the mystery surrounding the Eucharist, the central act of the Mass. The Grail derives from the dish in which Christ broke bread at the Last Supper, the strange bleeding lance which accompanied the Grail from the Holy Lance, with which Longinus pierced Christ's side as he hung on the Cross. Perceval, the pure and innocent hero, is intended as the archetype of religious knight-hood. A new goal was set, transcending that of courtly love, in which the knight-errant, once seeking fame and the love of his lady, now sought the sight of the Grail. Lancelot, for his secular virtues, was able to see the Grail but not to approach it; and even the sight of it so overwhelmed him that he lay unconscious for weeks afterwards. Clearly, in terms of religious knighthood, he was no longer the best knight in the world; and in some versions of the story Perceval replaces him. But Perceval's own history was by no means entirely one of innocence, and he in turn was replaced by Lancelot's son Galahad.

However, one of the greatest romances has Perceval alone as the Grail hero, and, furthermore, it is a German romance, which underlines some of the differences of approach between French and German chivalric writers. This is Wolfram von Eschenbach's *Parzival*, an unusual romance in that the author claimed to be a man of little learning when it came to writing such things down, and implies that he is merely a knight and a poet, not a clerk. Even if his artistic skill belies his claim to be almost illiterate, his work is one of the few which was certainly written by a knight. Yet the changes of emphasis are not what we would expect. Parzival (Perceval) becomes a much more complex and human figure, the marvels of Chrétien's tale are balanced by a strongly moral sequence of cause and effect, and the virtue which is most emphasised is *triuwe*, literally loyalty, but here extended to mean devotion, faith in love, and even the grace and love of God. Man's proper relationship with his fellow-beings and with God is thus governed by the one peculiarly knightly virtue. So we find Parzival happily married almost at the beginning of his adventures; the achievement of his quest brings as reward reunion with his lady, rather than union with her for the first time. Earthly love is subordinate to the spiritual quest, the striving towards fulfilment of his own nature. The description of the Grail castle clearly reflects the ideals and organisation of the military orders of knighthood such as the Templars; but it is interesting that Wolfram does not insist that Parzival should conform to their rule of celibacy, taking the broader view that man's nature should not be restrained, but directed aright. The final image is one of chivalry as the fulfilment of a natural nobility of spirit, a bond which links religion, love and knightly service. Wolfram gives to the material he uses an entirely new profundity; he never preaches or forces an artificial idealism on to his characters, but convincingly portrays Parzival as both human and heroic.

Parzival's stature is underlined by the two contrasting secondary heroes, Gawain and Feirefiz. Gawain appears in his familiar role as a courtly knight and ardent lover, but even he is happily married by the end of the poem; courtly love or *minne* is brought within the circle of ordinary human

(opposite) *Scenes
from Wolfram von
Eschenbach's version of
the Grail story,* Parzival

relationships which Wolfram values so highly; he emphasises kinship and inherited virtues throughout the poem, and if Gawain is not spiritually great enough to play a part in the Grail castle, he can at least achieve *triuwe* in love. Feirefiz is a character of Wolfram's own invention, son of Parzival's father Gahmuret by a heathen queen, strangely striped black and white. Like Gawain, he is a formidable knight, but he only achieves his full stature after his baptism, at which the stripes disappear and he becomes as fair as his half-brother. Gawain represents worldliness, Feirefiz estrangement from God. Just as Parzival fights both Gawain and Feirefiz (without recognising them) before he can finally ask the question that heals the Grail king, so he must overcome his worldly nature and his doubts about God before he can reach spiritual fulfilment.

It is difficult to do justice to the richness of Wolfram's poem; analysis makes it seem dry and theoretical, while it is, in fact, both profoundly spiritual and one of the liveliest and most appealing of the romances. As with the *minnesänger* and courtly love, the German poet has outstripped the formalities of chivalry to offer ideals which transcend those of chivalry in its ordinary sense.

Yet in the end the anonymous French romance writers were able to transcend their material as well, in the figures of Galahad, the 'knight of heaven', in the *Quest of the Holy Grail*, and of Arthur, the tragic king, in *The Death of King Arthur*. The author of the *Quest of the Holy Grail* seems to have been strongly influenced by the ideals of the Cistercian order of monks. The marvels and adventures now become real or symbolic tests of the aptitude of the knights for their spritual mission, and the Grail is clearly identified as a religious symbol; in the final scene, when the three knights who have achieved the quest are served with the Grail at the castle of Corbenic, its Christian meaning is expounded in noble and moving rhetoric. The *Quest of the Holy Grail* is indeed a sermon disguised as a romance, in which hermits are always ready to interpret a dream or an event in religious terms. Of the three knights who achieve the quest, Bors is the least worthy, but the most interesting character. He has sinned but against his will, and earns his redemption; and he is able to move at ease both in Arthur's court and at the Grail castle. Perceval retains his air of simplicity, here overlaid with holiness, so that he moves through danger and temptation as if unaware of their existence. Galahad, for whom 'all adventures draw back and make way' is too perfect a figure to arouse our sympathy, though he shows tenderness towards his father Lancelot. In Jean Frappier's words he is 'a highly stylised but not a desiccated character, the culmination of the effort to fuse chivalry with religion.' Lancelot, from whom Galahad inherits his earthly prowess, becomes the type of the reluctant sinner, and even though his repentance proves to be only temporary, he is vouchsafed a sight of the holy vessel.

How far we have come from Celtic marvels and knightly deeds-at-arms can best be illustrated by Malory's version of the end of the quest, where the central ritual of the Christian religion becomes the fulfilment of chivalrous aspirations:

So with that they heard the chamber door open, and there they saw angels; and two bore candles of wax, and the third bore a towel, and the fourth a spear which bled marvellously, that the drops fell within a box which he held with his other hand. And anon they set the candles upon the table, and the third the towel upon the Holy Grail, and the fourth the holy spear even upright upon the vessel.

And then the bishop made seeming as though he would have gone about the consecration of a Mass, and then he took a wafer which was made in the likeness of bread. And at the lifting up there came a figure in likeness of a child and the visage was as red and as bright as any fire, and smote himself into the bread, that all they saw it that the bread was formed of a fleshly man. And then he put it in the vessel again, and then he did what befitted a priest to do Mass.

And then he went to Sir Galahad and kissed him, and bade him go and kiss his fellows. And so he did anon. 'Now,' said he, 'the servants of Jesus Christ, ye shall be fed before this table with sweet meats that never knights yet tasted.'

And when he had said, he vanished away. And they sat them at the table in great dread and made their prayers. Then looked they and saw a man come out of the holy vessel that had all the signs of the Passion of Jesus Christ bleeding all openly and said:

'My knights and my servants and my true children, which have come out of deadly life into the spiritual life, I will no longer cover me from you, but ye shall see now a part of my secrets and my hidden things. Now holdeth and receiveth the high order and meat which ye have so much desired.'

Then took He himself the holy vessel and came to Sir Galahad. And he kneeled down and received his Saviour. And after him so received all his fellows, and they thought it so sweet that it was marvellous to tell. Then said He to Sir Galahad,

'Son, knowest thou what I hold between my hands?' 'No,' said he, 'unless you tell me.'

'This is,' said He, 'the holy dish wherein I ate the lamb on Easter Day, and now hast thou seen that which thou most desired to see. But yet hast thou not seen it so openly as thou shalt see it in the city of Sarras, in the spiritual palace. Therefore thou must go hence and bear with thee this holy vessel, for this night it shall depart from the realm of Logres and it shall nevermore be seen here.'

The Grail quest ends on a subdued note after these ecstatic heights: Perceval and Galahad die in the service of the Grail, and Bors is left to carry the tale of their achievement back to Arthur and his court, a court sadly depleted by the loss of many knights who had set out and failed to return. The closing book of the story of Arthur concentrates more on Lancelot and Guinevere, but also returns to Arthur himself.

Arthur's part in chivalric literature is an ambiguous one: he is essentially a warrior rather than a knight-errant, a fighter of battles rather than jousts. So for much of the time he is merely part of the setting, the patron whose generosity and nobility has created the Round Table. As such, he is the ideal king from the knight's point of view, putting chivalry before all else. His court is not concerned with the mundane business of running a kingdom, but only with high adventures; nor do

the knights have to seek favours and estates in order to live, but exist in a kind of dreamworld, remote from reality. Arthur's function, therefore, is largely formal: chivalry, always individualistic in real life, is represented in the romances almost entirely in terms of knight-errantry. So warfare proper is not part of the main body of the Arthurian romances, and indeed would be out of place among the quests, adventures and tournaments.

However, the framework of the Arthurian romances remains the history of Arthur himself, as told by Geoffrey of Monmouth; and the events of his career alter only slightly between Geoffrey's *History of the Kings of Britain* in the twelfth century, and Malory's *Le Morte Darthur* in the fifteenth century. The development is chiefly in Arthur's character: in Geoffrey he is an active leader who spends most of his reign on the battlefield, while in Malory his early successes are recorded and he moves on to his true chivalric function of patron of the Round Table. The image which predominates is a passive one, of someone borne along on the current of events rather than actively directing their course. This is underlined by the

Arthur's last battle against Mordred; note the cart bearing the standards, which would serve as a rallying point

metaphor of the Wheel of Fortune: Arthur is seen as a figure seated on a great wheel turned by Fortune, rising up to the highest point of the wheel and then dashed headlong to the ground. It is a fatalistic view which, none the less, in the hands of an artist of Malory's standing becomes an intense tragedy. The ruler of the court whose knights achieved the spiritual heights of the Grail is betrayed by the earthly sin of Lancelot and Guinevere, and by his own nephew. The Round Table disintegrates in a welter of petty jealousies, tragic mistakes, and misplaced loyalty. Arthur meets his mysterious end almost alone, the great company either dead around him or dispersed. No one pronounces an eloquent lament for him as Ector does for Lancelot: for Arthur's virtues are not those of the chivalric world. He is the link between the knights whom he leads and the world of romance itself; his death, surrounded by mystery, becomes an adventure, a release from the terrors and tragedies of his last days.

Without the controlling and shaping theme of Arthur and the Round Table and its associated heroes, whose stories were fixed in broad outline, the chivalric romance became verbose and self-indulgent, piling marvel on marvel without any real thread or purpose. This had happened in the most extended versions of Arthurian romance, but the framework survived intact; without such limitations, and with a chivalric hero at the centre, there was no reason to bring the sequence of episodes to a close. In Cervantes' *Don Quixote*, a book as full of shrewd common sense as of madcap misadventures, the canon of Toledo has this to say about the later romances:

> For they presented a broad and spacious field through which the pen could run without let or hindrance, describing shipwrecks, tempests, encounters and battles; painting a brave captain with all the features necessary for the part; showing his wisdom in forestalling his enemies' cunning, his eloquence in persuading or dissuading his soldiers, his ripeness in counsel, his prompt resolution, his courage in awaiting or in making an attack; now depicting a tragic and lamentable incident, now a joyful and unexpected event; here a most beautiful lady, chaste, intelligent, and modest; there a Christian knight, valiant, and gentle; in one place a monstrous, barbarous braggart; in another a courteous prince, brave and wise; representing the goodness and loyalty of vassals, and the greatness and generosity of lords. Sometimes the writer might show his knowledge of astrology, or his excellence at cosmography or as

a musician, or his wisdom in affairs of state, and he might even have an opportunity of showing his skill in necromancy.

He goes on to say that despite these opportunities, the result has been 'notorious nonsense, monsters without feet or head'. Just as chivalry had begun to lose its place in the real world, so it began to be a relic of the literary past. Aspiring authors in the sixteenth century looked to classical literature for their models, and although the romances remained popular throughout Europe – as the enormous number of early printed editions bear witness – they were no longer a living form.

The romances were not the only form of chivalric literature. The influence of chivalry is clearly visible in many works that we would now class as historical, which deal with real events and often report them accurately. The chivalric element lies in the writer's attitude to his material, and from the twelfth century onwards there are numerous examples. We have already looked at the biography of William Marshal and the poem which describes the tournament at Chauvency in 1285; Ulrich von Lichtenstein's account of his jousts in Austria and Italy is a more extreme example of the genre. The *History of William Marshal* does indeed become serious history towards the middle of the poem, and is concerned with English politics instead of French tournaments for well over half its length. But its view of politics is not coloured by chivalry; for an example of this we have to move on to the fourteenth century, to the 'chronicler of chivalry' Jean Froissart and his circle. Froissart's model, from whom he borrowed much of the first books of' his chronicle almost verbatim, was another worldly canon, Jean Le Bel of Liège. Le Bel had a brother who was a knight, and lived in lordly style himself; even though his family were citizens rather than aristocrats. He accompanied Edward III on his Scottish campaigns in 1327, so he had first-hand experience of warfare. His main concern is not with the events of his time, but with their protagonists. Here is his account of the battle of Sluys in 1340:

> The French had two and a half times as many ships as their opponents, including the great ship called the Christopher which was able to destroy many smaller vessels and did much damage to the English; without God's help they would have had neither strength nor spirit to resist the French. But King Edward bore himself nobly and did such great deeds of prowess with his own body that he cheered and gave heart to all the others by his

own courage, and by that of the Earl of Derby and Sir Walter Mauny, who bore himself very well there, as did several others whose names I do not know; and – chiefly by the grace of God – the French, Normans, Gascons, Bretons and Genoese were eventually killed, drowned and defeated, and few of them escaped.

There is no mention of tactics or equipment, or of the part played by the English archers and seamen, in what was a complex and drawn out battle. Instead, three noble figures are mentioned: substitute Arthur, Lancelot and Gawain and it could easily be a passage from the part of the romances dealing with Arthur's campaigns. Froissart takes Le Bel as his starting point, and roundly declares the object of his work in the preface to his *Chronicles*:

> That the honourable enterprises, noble adventures, and deeds of arms, performed in the wars between England and France, may be properly related, and held in perpetual remembrance – to the end that brave men taking example from them may be encouraged in their well-doing, I sit down to record a history deserving great praise. . .

Froissart had written poetry and romances before he came to write chronicles, and a romantic attitude to chivalry colours his pages, even though he also conveys a great deal of factual information: his account of Sluys, for instance, has considerable detail about the manoeuvres during the battle and the details of the fighting. He is a historian in the sense that he values factual information and often tries to interpret and illuminate his facts; but his actual purpose in writing the *Chronicles* was literary and chivalric. In the vast bulk of his work there are long passages on politics, but the memorable episodes are those where chivalry comes to the fore, as in Sir Walter Manny's skirmish with those besieging Hennebont, or in the famous and probably apocryphal gesture of the Black Prince towards his captive, King John of France, after the Battle of Poitiers in 1356:

> And the Prince served before the King's table and all the other tables, as humbly as he could; nor would he by any means sit at the King's table, however much the King requested it, saying that he was far from being worthy of sitting at table with so great a Prince and such a valiant man as he had shown himself to be that day. And he constantly kneeled to the King and said: 'Dear lord, do not be so downcast, even though God has not

granted your wishes today; because my lord father will certainly honour and befriend you as best he can and will make an agreement with you in such reasonable terms that you and he will always be good friends. Indeed I think you have good reason to be cheerful, even if things have gone against you, because you have won a great name for prowess today, and have outdone your own greatest knights. I do not say this to flatter you; everyone on our side who saw how each one fought agreed about this and award you the prize and garland if you will wear them.'

Again, Froissart explains how in 1388 he considered 'that great deeds of arms would not happen for a long while in the borders of Picardy and in Flanders, because there was peace there,' so for fear of idleness he set off to visit the Count of Foix at Orthez in the foothills of the Pyrenees, gathering news as he went. The Count made him welcome, and readily answered his questions, 'saying that the history I was employed on would in times to come be more sought after than any other, 'because,' he added, 'more gallant deeds of arms have been performed within these last fifty years, and more wonderful things have happened, than for three hundred years before.' With this encouragement, Froissart set to work and gathered much information, which, he says, he will set down 'to give examples to these worthies who wish to advance themselves in renown. If I have heretofore dwelt on gallant deeds, attacks and captures, of castles, towns and forts, on hard-fought battles and skirmishes, many more will now ensue; all of which, by God's grace, I will truly narrate.'

Even the form of his history is similar to that of a romance; instead of dividing the work into the chronicles of separate areas, he practises a technique like the 'interlacing' of the romances, a device whereby a number of separate plots can be kept going, where one knight's adventures are described for several pages, and the scene switches abruptly elsewhere, with a brief phrase such as 'Now leave we Sir Gawain, and turn unto Sir Lancelot . . .'. Froissart moves with similar phrases between Spain and Flanders, Savoy and Scotland, reminding his readers of the thread he now picks up by saying 'You have heard before how . . .'. Another indication of Froissart's chivalric bias is the extensive treatment he gives to that staple of romance, the tournament. The jousts held at St Inglevert in 1389 occupy almost as much space as the events surrounding the Battle of Poitiers; indeed, if we take the battle itself, the jousts are reported in far more detail.

Froissart's chronicles, however, differ sharply from the romances in one respect: they have no heroes as such. Even such obvious candidates as the Black Prince are not treated as protagonists on whom the story centres, and there is no eulogy of the Prince's deeds, except in the reporting of favourable comments by others. Instead, Froissart's admiration for chivalry emerges in his emphasis on events; the matter of his chronicle is made to approximate as closely as possible to that of romance, but the substance is none the less political and historical.

The romances offered the knight a vision of life as it might have been; Froissart gave him a picture of life as it was through knightly eyes; and our last group of authors aimed to instruct him in life as it should be, by means of manuals on how a knight should behave. The most popular of these was *The Book of the Order of Chivalry* written by a distinguished Spanish philosopher, Ramon Llull. Llull's adventurous and sometimes eccentric career began with a knightly, upbringing in Majorca (where he was born, in about 1235), and he led a conventional, even dissipated, life until a religious crisis at the age of thirty-one led him to missionary and philosophical work. He spent twenty years learning and teaching Arabic and philosophy, and from 1291 onwards he made a series of expeditions to North Africa in order to preach Christianity to the Moslems. On his third such expedition, at the age of nearly eighty, he was stoned to death by furious Moslems outside the town of Bougie. He was later made a saint, despite his somewhat erratic and unorthodox philosophical treatises. Altogether, he was an unlikely candidate for the authorship of the most popular work on chivalry of the Middle Ages; but his treatise, originally written in Catalan, exists in numerous French manuscripts, in two Scottish versions, and in a translation by Caxton published in 1484, the year before his famous edition of Malory.

The Book of the Order of Chivalry was written in 1275–6, when Llull was forty, and after his conversion. It is a learned book, and chivalry is duly explained with reference to the religious idea of knighthood which we shall come to in the next chapter. But it is also a lively piece of writing, well calculated to appeal to the knights themselves just as much as to Llull's fellow-scholars discussing theories of education. The book opens with a picture of the 'good hermit knight' who is to be Llull's spokesman:

> It once happened in a country that there was a wise knight, who had
> long sustained the order of knighthood and who by his nobility and

strength and high courage and wisdom, and by risking his life, had been through wars, jousts and tournaments, and had had many noble and glorious victories in battle. Because, brave though he was, he realised that he could no longer live as he had done in the past and was approaching his end, he chose to live as a hermit, for his natural virtues were undermined by old age, and he no longer had the strength or will to use weapons as he had been accustomed to do.

The other character in the book is a young squire, on his way to the castle where a great king is holding his winter court, at which he hopes to be made a knight. He falls asleep on horseback, and his horse strays off the road to the hermitage. The hermit knight, learning of his intention to seek knighthood, offers to instruct him in the ways of chivalry, and gives him a little book on the subject, which is, of course, the book that Llull proceeds to write.

What follows may seem to us a curious mixture of fiction, invented traditions and fragments of history, but medieval writers did not like to serve up their theories without a suitable veneer of traditional authority. So we learn that knights were originally chosen, one for each thousand men, to uphold justice; the horse was chosen as their steed because it was 'the most suitable, handsome, and swift, best able to work and most apt to serve men'. Because knighthood was a noble institution, knights were given all the best armour. Llull goes on to emphasise the links between nobility and knighthood, and makes the point that an evil knight is far worse than an ordinary man who turns to wickedness, because a knight has been chosen to guard society, and is betraying the trust placed in him by lesser men. Llull sees the knight as someone who will inspire terror in ordinary people, so that they will be afraid to do wrong, a kind of old-fashioned police force. But alongside these idealistic views of knighthood, he also acknowledges that a knight has to learn special skills, the skills that Gornemanz once taught Perceval, just as a carpenter must learn his trade.

This mixture of theory and practice continues as Llull embroiders his theme. He lists the knight's duties, emphasising his high calling and his important function in society, but then goes on to themes nearer to a knight's heart:

A knight should ride warhorses, joust, go to tournaments, hold Round Tables, hunt stags and rabbits, bears, lions and similar creatures: these things are a knight's duty because to do them exercises a knight in the practice of arms and accustoms him to maintain the order of knighthood.

To despise and to neglect things by which a knight is made more fit for his duties is to despise and neglect knighthood itself.

But Llull goes on to warn that mere bodily strength and boldness are not enough to make a good knight: sense and spirit are needed as well. He then sets out a form of catechism for the squire who wishes to become a knight. He emphasises again true courage as the knight's first virtue:

Seek not noble courage in speech, for speech is not always truth; seek it not in rich clothes, for many a fine habit conceals cowardice, treachery and evil; seek it not in your horse, for he cannot speak to you; seek it not in fine harness and equipment for they too often hide an evil and cowardly heart. Seek noble courage in faith, hope, charity, justice, strength, moderation and loyalty . . .

Knighthood has nothing to do with physical beauty, and a squire must be of mature age before he can become a knight; but good ancestry from a noble line is essential, since this is simply 'ancient and continual honour'. Some degree of wealth is also needed, lest the new knight turn to evil ways simply in order to make ends meet or even just to pay for his equipment. Llull would also exclude any squire, however high his birth or great his virtues, who was in any way deformed, a restriction which would seem out of keeping with his emphasis on spiritual rather than physical qualities.

Llull goes on to describe the ceremony of knighting, and then returns to his theme of knightly virtue. Here the hermit takes over from the knight: for this is a straightforward sermon, illustrated with Biblical examples, belonging to the literature of religion rather than chivalry. He ends, however, on a worldly note, describing the honour due to a knight and his rank in society: 'any noble baron or lord who does honour to a knight in his court and in his council and at his table, does honour to himself.' He briefly mentions a knight's relations with women, but only to say that just as a knight's wife should not have children by a commoner, so a knight should not have a common mistress, lest he destroy the purity of his line – a far cry from the troubadours and their high ideal of love! But Llull is writing in a very different tradition, one which pays some respect to the ideal of knighthood as portrayed in the romances, but which really leads us to our next topic, chivalry in relation to religion.

Chivalry and Religion

Geoffrey Charny, writing his manual on knighthood in the fourteenth century, saw knighthood and priesthood as the two great orders of the Church. Yet originally knighthood was a purely secular arrangement, with no religious overtones. Such a development would seem strange to us today, but the Church in the Middle Ages saw itself as all embracing, concerned very directly with the humblest details of everyday life. So, just as the fisherman had his nets blessed or the farmer his seed-corn, the knight's sword was blessed. From the eleventh century onwards there is evidence that bishops were present at knighting ceremonies, and from the mid-tenth century comes a prayer to be said over a knight's sword just after he has been knighted, which runs:

> Hearken, we beseech Thee, O Lord, to our prayers, and deign to bless with the right hand of thy majesty this sword with which this Thy servant desires to be girded, that it may be a defence of churches, widows, orphans and all Thy servants against the scourge of the pagans, that it may be the terror and dread of other evildoers, and that it may be just both in attack and defence.

This, however, in no way set the knight apart from the rest of society, and gave him no special status in the Church. A later prayer sets the knights apart from the common people and makes of them a kind of secular arm of the Church:

> O Lord who established three degrees of mankind after the Fall in the whole world, that thy faithful people might dwell in peace and secure from all

onslaughts of evil, hear our prayers and grant that thy servant may use this sword, which by thy grace we bless and give to him and gird on him, to repel the hosts who besiege God's church and to defend himself with thy protection against all his foes.

By the fourteenth century the simple form of blessing had developed into a special service and, like many great Church ceremonies, was usually followed by a lavish feast. Geoffrey Charny describes the elaborate procedures and symbolism:

> When someone is to be knighted, he should first of all confess his sins and put himself into a fit state to receive communion. And on the eve of the day when he is to be knighted, he should wash and cleanse his body of all the filth of sin and evil living, and leave this filth behind in the water. So he should get out of the bath cleansed in conscience by the water, and should go and lie in a brand-new bed with clean white sheets and should rest there like one who has come through great travails against sin and many torments by devils. And the bed signifies the sound sleep of conscience when it has appeased our Lord for all that it has done in the past

The ceremonial of making of a knight: girding with a sword, robing, and presentation of a banner

to anger him. Then the knights should come to the bed to dress him; and he should be dressed in new linen clothing and everything else should be new; just as his body has been washed of filth and sin, so the new clothes signify that he should keep himself clean and spotless of sin in future. Then he should be dressed by the knights in scarlet robes, signifying that he is sworn to shed his blood for the faith of Our Lord and to defend and maintain the laws of Holy Church. And then the knights should bring black hose, as symbol that he came from earth, and to earth he must return, and that he must expect to die, nor can he know the hour of his death, and so he must trample on all pride. Then the knights should bring a white girdle and gird it on him, as a sign that he should always be surrounded by chastity and cleanliness. Then the knights bring a scarlet cloak and put it on his shoulders as a sign of humility, for such cloaks were always in the old days signs of humility. Then the knights lead him joyfully to the church, where he must remain all night and keep vigil all night until dawn in deep devotion and praying to our Lord to forgive his evil sleeping and waking in the past, and to make him always watchful in his service thereafter. The next day the knights take him to hear Mass devoutly, praying to our Lord for grace to enter the order [of knighthood] and to maintain it in His service and grace. And when Mass has been sung and said, the knights shall bring him to the knight who is to confer the order on him. This knight shall put a gilded spur on his foot, signifying that just as gold is the most coveted metal, so it is put on his foot to take away all covetousness from his heart. Then the knight who is to give him the order of knighthood takes a sword [and girds it on him]; just as the sword has two cutting edges, so he must keep and sustain and maintain right, reason and justice on all sides and never betray the Christian faith or the rights of Holy Church. Then the other knight kisses him in confirmation of the order he is bestowing, as a sign of peace and love and loyalty, which he should always seek out wherever he may rightly do so. And then that knight gives him the accolade, a blow which signifies that he must always remember the order of knighthood which he has received and must perform the deeds which belong to the order of knighthood. And in this manner these things are and should be done.

Charny is describing the kind of ceremony in which a great lord's son would take part in peacetime. Knighthood was not always so elaborately granted, and it was always the religious part of the ceremony that was omitted when knights were given the order during a war. In many ways this knighting on the battlefield seems to have carried more prestige, particularly as it was often a reward for valour. But the Church did its best to take part in this important moment in a knight's life, and it also tried to promote the idea of knighthood as an institution with religious meaning through sermons and even through romances. In the *Prose Lancelot*, the Lady of the Lake gives Lancelot a long lecture on the qualities of a knight, and describes the way in which the knight's armour symbolises his duty to the Church. As a knight's hauberk guards his body, so a knight must safeguard the Church. As his helmet protects his head, so a knight must defend the Church. As his lance terrifies the unarmed mob, so he must drive off the enemies of the Church. The two edges of his sword show that he serves both God and people, while the point shows that all people must obey him; the horse on which he rides likewise represents the people, whom the knight must guide but who must in return support him and give him the wherewithal to lead an honourable life.

The practical effect of these exhortations was insignificant: the full-scale service and ceremonies of knighthood were only experienced by a minority of knights. The Church could explain and encourage knighthood in Christian terms, but in practical terms the business of knights was as mundane as that of farmers or fishermen – and inherently rather more sinful. The Church had great difficulty in coming to terms with warfare, as its early history and tradition was almost entirely pacifist. Eventually St Augustine made the distinction, borrowed from the lawyers, between just war and sinful war, and fighting men were thus able to take their place within the Church. Equally, as the Church became a political as well as a spiritual power, it had its own wars to fight; and it was here that it was at last able to make a real impression on the life of the ordinary knight, and to offer him both a real adventure and a Christian quest, as arduous as anything in the romances.

Pilgrimage was an important part of religious life in the Middle Ages. Whether out of simple devotion or as penance, crowds of men and women made their way to the great shrines of Europe to pay homage to the saints or to holy places. In the early Middle Ages the most important of these routes were those to Santiago de Compostela in Spain, to Rome itself and, most arduous of all, to Jerusalem. Despite the immense hardships of the latter

journey, involving either dangerous miles through the deserts of Asia Minor
or the rigours of a sea-voyage in primitive ships, Christian pilgrims from
Western Europe thronged to Jerusalem. In 1064-5 we hear of a party said to
be seven thousand strong travelling to Jerusalem; and many nobles and even
kings of the period either went on or planned a journey to the Holy City.
Access to the holy places, which had been in Moslem hands since the seventh
century, was unhindered until the beginning of the eleventh century, when
the reigning Caliph, Hakim, suddenly began to persecute the Christians and
in 1009 tore down the Church of the Holy Sepulchre. But even his courtiers
came to regard this as the work of a madman when he declared himself
divine in 1016, and his persecutions were soon directed towards Moslems
rather than Christians. Freedom of access was restored by 1020, but the
growing chaos in the Near East made pilgrimage more difficult.

In 1095, the Emperor of Byzantium, Alexius, sent an embassy to the Pope
with the aim of obtaining Christian knights to help him to reconquer eastern
Turkey which the Byzantines had lost to the Seldjuk Turks after the
disastrous battle of Manzikert in 1071. The Seldjuks, nomadic tribesmen
from central Asia, were the cause of the unsettled state of the Near East, and
their rapidly growing empire was a threat not only to Byzantium but to the
older Moslem dynasties who had been tolerant of Christian pilgrimages.
Alexius' envoys, concerned to make their appeal as dramatic as possible,
painted a picture of impending doom for the Church in the East, describing
Jerusalem itself as threatened. Their Western hearers, unfamiliar with the
complex politics of the area, fastened on the one concept that they could
understand: the Holy City was about to be desecrated by the unbelievers and
must be rescued. The Pope himself had a clearer understanding of what was
at stake, and his first appeal, launched at Clermont in France in November
1095, was in fact a plea for help to be sent to the Church in the East. His
speech was publicised in advance as an important one, and the audience was
so huge that it had to be delivered in a field outside the town. The gist of his
message, put forward with great eloquence, was that here was an opportunity
for the knights of the West, instead of fighting each other and oppressing the
poor, to earn glory in heaven by going to the aid of their fellow Christians in
the East. It was to be both pilgrimage and war on God's behalf. His message
was received with great enthusiasm, and his hearers flocked to 'take the
cross', to pledge themselves to the expedition by wearing the badge of a cross
on their shoulder. In the course of the next months, the general and rather

vague object of the expedition crystallised: its object was to free Jerusalem from the heathen. This was not at all what Alexius' envoys had intended, nor indeed did Jerusalem particularly need to be freed while pilgrims could still come and go as they pleased; but the goal had been set, and it increased yet further the power of Pope Urban's appeal.

Whether by accident or by deep design, Urban had indeed hit on an idea which struck a responsive chord in the knights of the West, as well as in their humbler followers. The Church, previously rather doubtful about their activities, opposed to private wars as later to tournaments, was now offering a practical way of serving God which was within any knight's grasp. For many knights, those younger sons without lands of their own, it also offered a chance to make a very material fortune; just as William Marshal, as a younger son, had made his way in the world by his skill at tournaments, so his counterpart going on crusade could hope for booty and, as it turned out, land. This was particularly attractive to knights from northern France and England, where only the eldest son could inherit and the younger sons had to find other lands by marrying an heiress, or had to go into the Church; but it was also attractive to those from the southern lands where inheritances were divided equally, because the repeated division of estates meant that noble families might be reduced in a few generations to little more than serfs. So the departure of some members of a family on crusade solved not only their own economic problems, but helped those who stayed behind.

But material rewards were not the prime object of the early crusaders. Urban had mentioned in his speech at Clermont the remission of all penances imposed by the Church for those who went on crusade. As the drive to recruit crusaders gathered momentum, he offered a new and better reward, the actual remission of sins in return for the good deed of crusading; this meant that not merely the penances, which might have saved the sinner from penalties in the after-life, but those actual penalties themselves would be avoided by crusaders. In later centuries this was to lead to all kinds of abuses, but its immediate effect was undoubtedly considerable. The many preachers who urged people to join the crusade used the theme repeatedly, and in the twelfth century St Bernard of Clairvaux compared it in one of his letters to a 'splendid bargain':

O mighty soldier, O man of war, you now have a cause for which you can fight without endangering your soul; a cause in which to win is glorious and for which to die is but gain. Or are you a shrewd businessman, a man quick to see the profits of this world? If you are, I can offer you a splendid bargain. Do not miss this opportunity. Take the sign of the cross. At once you will have indulgence for all the sins which you confess with a contrite heart. It does not cost you much to buy and if you wear it with humility you will find that it is worth the kingdom of heaven.

Enthusiasm alone was not enough to get the crusading armies to Jerusalem, though many poor folk, fired by the preachers' enthusiastic eloquence, tried to make their way there; the largest of these ramshackle armies led by the popular orator Peter the Hermit and a knight called Walter (nicknamed 'the Penniless'), travelled as far as Byzantium, where its disorderly conduct deeply disturbed the Byzantine government. The Emperor Alexius had hoped for well-trained mercenaries from the West; what arrived was a horde of lightly armed, ill-disciplined infantry, who were massacred at their first encounter with the Turks on 21 October 1096. The other contingents of the People's Crusade, having turned aside to conduct vicious attacks on the Jewish communities in the Rhineland, never reached Byzantium.

These, however, were unofficial crusades, and very few knights took part in them. The crusade proper, led by the papal legate, Adhémar Bishop of Le Puy, and Count Raymond IV of Toulouse, was slower in getting started, but when it eventually left in four groups, from August 1096 onwards, it was at least properly equipped. The main body reached Byzantium at the end of April 1097; the contingents led by Godfrey, Lord of Bouillon, and Bohemund of Taranto, from Flanders and southern Italy respectively, arrived some weeks earlier, while that led by Robert of Flanders arrived at the beginning of May. Once at Byzantium, the first obstacle to the crusaders' plans materialised. Their aims were, as we have seen, very different from those for which the Emperor Alexius had launched his appeal. What had started as a move to rescue the Byzantine possessions in the East had become an expedition aimed at a goal which had no military significance: but Jerusalem and the lands around it were still regarded as part of their empire by the Byzantines. So instead of a simple campaign against the Seldjuk Turks, the Emperor found himself with an independent third force in the area; and the crusaders, moreover, showed every sign of wishing to hold their conquests

The emperor Frederick Barbarossa, one of the leaders of the First Crusade, in crusader garb

independently of him. Alexius therefore used his control of shipping across the Bosphorus and of food supplies to force the leading crusaders to swear either oaths of allegiance or at least oaths to respect his possessions. Even Raymond of Toulouse, who at first declared that he had come only in God's service, duly took the oath. It was an ominous warning of things to come, that the splendid simplicity of the crusaders' zeal could not operate in a political vacuum, and that awareness of political reality was as important to success as spiritual enthusiasm.

Nonetheless, when the army set out again from Byzantium, they needed all their zeal to keep them on their way to Jerusalem. Despite two victories over the Turks, at Nicaea, and near Dorylaeum in Anatolia, their progress was very slow. After Nicaea, one of their leaders wrote that they hoped to be in Jerusalem in five weeks, that is, at the end of June 1097. As it was, they only reached Antioch at the end of October, while the important Norman contingent had taken another route, further east, where they had taken the cities of Tarsus and Edessa. Here Baldwin, Count of Boulogne, at the head of part of the Norman and Flemish contingent established himself as ruler, and his part in the crusade came to an end. Needless to say, he did not regard himself as in any way bound to the Byzantine Emperor, but instead founded the first Frankish state in the East.

Antioch was the key to Syria, and it was essential to take it before moving on. The siege took seven months, but the crusaders, their numbers severely reduced by the hardships of the winter, having taken the city, immediately found themselves besieged by a Moslem force which had come to relieve the town. At this crucial juncture, a miraculous discovery was made in the cathedral: a member of the army, Peter Bartholomew, had a vision that the Holy Lance, with which Christ's side was pierced at the Crucifixion, was buried in the cathedral. It was duly found, and morale immediately rose. The episode was probably stage-managed, and the legate Adhémar remained sceptical throughout: he had, after all, seen the Holy Lance at Byzantium. But it shows that there were men in the army objective enough to realise exactly how the ordinary knight's zeal might be aroused again, and how essential the religious element in the crusade was to the success of the expedition. A fortnight later, the besieging Moslems were routed by a desperate sortie led by Bohemund, and Antioch was secure in Christian hands. A new menace, in the shape of plague, which carried off Adhémar of Le Puy and many others, now appeared; and it was not until January of the following year that agreement was reached on the future of Antioch. Bohemund, after much wrangling, became its prince in return for a promise to continue to Jerusalem with the rest of the army, a bargain which he promptly failed to keep.

The march southwards began on 13 January 1099. Raymond of Toulouse led his troops out of Antioch, barefoot and dressed as a pilgrim, in an attempt to remind his fellow commanders of their original crusading vows. His men met little resistance on the way, as the local rulers were disorganised and anxious to avoid trouble. Jerusalem itself, however, lay within the territory of the Fatimid caliphs of Egypt, far more powerful opponents, and even though their first month in Fatimid territory went virtually without an engagement, the crusaders came within sight of Jerusalem on 7 June 1099, only to find its gates shut and the city well provided for a siege. The Egyptians had, in fact, recovered the city from the Turks only a year before, and were well aware of the problems of the besiegers.

In the first flush of enthusiasm the crusaders attempted to scale the walls without adequate equipment on 13 June and were driven back. The city had powerful defences, the site was inherently strong, and Romans, Greeks and Egyptians in turn had enlarged and maintained its massive walls. There was little water or supplies to be had in the barren land around the city, and the wells had been poisoned by order of the governor of Jerusalem before the army arrived. There was little apparent hope of obtaining nails, and bolts and ropes to make siege machines, and almost no timber to be had. But four days after the abortive assault, six Christian ships with the very supplies that were needed reached Jaffa: and by extended foraging raids the crusaders managed to gather together the wood they needed. Two great siege-castles and other apparatus slowly took shape; but it was now the height of summer, and to make matters worse, news came of an army setting out from Egypt to relieve the city.

Once again, the last hope was to arouse the fervour of the men and to attempt a desperate assault. Adhémar of Le Puy was said to have appeared in a vision to a priest and to have ordered the crusaders to hold a fast and to go in procession barefoot around the walls. If they did this, and did it with truly pious hearts; the city would be theirs within nine days. The fast was duly ordered, and was strictly observed for three days; and on the second day a great procession made its way round the walls, at the end of which the finest preachers in the army harangued the men. Five days later, on the evening of 13 July, while the army's zeal was still aroused, the order was given for a general assault. For a whole day the crusaders fought to bring up their siege-towers; one reached the walls, but its men were unable to get on to the wall. On the morning of 15 July, the other tower, manned by Godfrey of Bouillon's men, was brought up and succeeded in getting a bridge across to the top of the wall. Scaling ladders were positioned against the walls near the siege tower; soon enough crusaders had entered the city to open the gates. By the afternoon the city was in Christian hands: but the moment of triumph was marred by a fearful bloodbath, in which the inhabitants of the city, Moslems and Jews alike, were indiscriminately cut down, until the streets ran with blood. The horror of this first act of fanaticism was to have long-drawn-out consequences for the future of the Christians in the East.

Once again, after the inspired victory, the crusaders were faced by down-to-earth problems which they had not considered, and for which they were ill-prepared. They had no real plans for the administration of the conquered city, and attempts to agree a course of action during the days preceding their victory had led only to quarrels. Eventually, Godfrey of Bouillon was chosen as 'defender of the Holy Sepulchre', but only after both he and Raymond of Toulouse had refused 'to wear a crown in the city where Christ had worn a crown of thorns'. It was almost with relief that the leaders of the crusaders, who were by now seriously at loggerheads, turned to the problem of the Egyptian army approaching from the south. Uniting their forces for the last time, they surprised and overwhelmed the Egyptians near Ascalon on 12 August.

The majority of the crusaders now made their way north, leaving Godfrey to hold Jerusalem with little more than a handful of men. Raymond, having failed to gain Jerusalem for himself, established himself at Tripoli some years later; other nobles joined Bohemund and Baldwin at Antioch and Edessa. On Godfrey's death in 1100, Baldwin became ruler of Jerusalem; he had no qualms about taking a royal title, and at his coronation on 25 December 1100, the Latin kingdom of Jerusalem was established.

The achievement of the first crusaders, wrought by a remarkable mixture of religious zeal and knightly skill, was astonishing. But it left behind an impractical kingdom, unable to support itself economically, short of fighting men, and opposed by potentially dangerous enemies. The land varied immensely in climate and fertility, and was difficult to exploit with the limited techniques of twelfth-century agriculture: furthermore, the hinterland was divided from the coast by a mountain range, so that communications were poor. Even given a well-organised administration, the problems were immense: but the crusaders had no plans for an organised settlement, and the establishment of the kingdom on a permanent basis was little short of a, miracle.

However, the lack of resources in the East, even taking into account the other crusader principalities strung out like a ribbon to the north, meant that in a crisis the only hope would be a renewed appeal to the Christians in the West. Partly from this realisation and partly out of a desire to embody the zeal of the First Crusade in a more permanent form, there arose the first of the military religious orders which were to play such a notable part in medieval European history. The beginnings were humble enough: the original idea was put forward by a knight from Champagne, Hugues de Payens, in the 1120s. Hugues de Payens and eight companions had been acting as guardians of pilgrims on the main route to Jerusalem, which ran from Jaffa to the Holy City, but was open to attack from the Egyptian fortress at Ascalon. They were encouraged by Baldwin II and were given quarters in the royal palace known as the Temple of Solomon. By 1123 their numbers seem to have increased, as Hugues was referred to as *'Magister militum Templi'*, master of the soldiers of the Temple. They were bound by an oath of poverty, obedience and chastity, and it was only a short step, therefore, to the idea of a group of knights living officially under monastic rule. In 1126 Hugues de Payens went to the West, his mission being to get a formal constitution approved by the Pope. In this he found an eager supporter in Bernard de Clairvaux, who wrote an eloquent pamphlet to further their cause, *De laude novae militiae* (*In Praise of the New Soldiery*), in which he took the secular knights of his day to task for the neglect of their true duties, and contrasted them with the ideal poverty and fervour of the proposed Templar order. In 1128 the Council of Troyes approved the rule submitted to them by Hugues de Payens; in its preamble, we can detect Bernard's hand in the attack on knights who 'despised the love of justice, which belonged to their duties, and did not do as they ought, that is, defend poor men, widows, orphans and the Church; but instead they competed to rape, despoil and murder.' The initial emphasis was on the converse of this, on protection and defence, both of pilgrims and of the holy places that were the object of their pilgrimage.

The Templars very quickly attracted widespread attention, and rich gifts were made to them. By the time of Hugues de Payens' death in 1136 they had substantial possessions in Western Europe, and had established 'provinces' in

Portugal (where they were given land as early as 1128), Aragon, Castile, England and France. They were also beginning to be an important force in Palestine. In the decades following Hugues' death, the idea of a military force within a religious order was imitated by the members of the Order of St John of Jerusalem (known as Hospitallers), who had originally cared for sick pilgrims, but had extended their work to their general welfare. At first knights were only admitted as lay brothers, but by the middle of the century they were entering the order as full monastic members, and its statutes were amended accordingly.

However, both the military orders were very small – if indeed the Hospitallers even existed – when the first great challenge to the new kingdom came. In 1145, the northernmost of the Christian states in the East, Edessa, fell to the Turkish leader Zengi, partly because the Christian barons were unable to make up their quarrels and unite on a common course of action. The shock of this major reverse did not improve their political sense, because in the following year they quarrelled with the one Moslem ruler friendly to them, Unur of Damascus. Faced with a threatened attack by Zengi's successor, Nur-ed-Din, they appealed to the West for help. The Second Crusade, led by Louis VII of France, reached Palestine in answer to

Crac des Chevaliers, one of the great fortresses of the Military Orders

*Two Templars on one
horse; a drawing by
Matthew Paris
emphasising the original
poverty of the order*

the appeal in March 1148. A German contingent had been slaughtered at
Dorylaeum, near the site of the First Crusade's victory, and the French
reached Antioch only after considerable hardships. If, once they had arrived,
their zeal had had an obvious target, all might have been well; but Bernard's
moving appeals to go out to help to save the holy places, made in some
distant Western field many months before, bore little relationship to the
realities of the situation. Caught in a web of quarrels, plots, distrust and
conflicting interests, the crusaders were bewildered at what they found. To
make matters worse, one of their leaders, the Count of Toulouse, died
suddenly, the Count of Tripoli reputedly having murdered him for fear that
he might claim the lands once ruled by his father, Raymond of Toulouse.
Louis, deeply pious, had expected to find some kind of permanent crusade
being waged in the East; instead, he found nobles who, like the lord who had
lost Edessa, were more like native princes than Christians. The conflict
between the interests of the crusaders, eager for action and spectacular

conquests, and the shrewder Frankish princes who knew that they had to live with their neighbours when the crusaders had returned home, was becoming apparent. The crusaders found that there was no clear objective; and when a target was at last chosen, it was the worst possible choice. Instead of following Raymond of Antioch's suggestion and attacking Nur-ed-Din's base at Aleppo, the crusaders and the Queen Regent of Jerusalem decided to continue the quarrel with Damascus, which could have been an ally. Furthermore, when they laid siege to the city, it proved more than able to resist them, and when Nur-ed-Din threatened to counter-attack, the crusaders had to retreat with heavy losses.

The contrast between the First and Second Crusades is very sharp, and the disastrous outcome of the latter was to influence all future crusades. In a sense, the crusading ideal was something which could be used effectively only once, when there was a clear objective and before the realities of everyday politics could intrude. The men of the First Crusade had a clear objective and almost no idea of the difficulties involved; the leaders of the Second Crusade, on the other hand, came to have all too clear an idea of the difficulties and little idea of their objective. The Third Crusade of 1191–2, launched after the disastrous defeat at Hattin in 1187 and the subsequent loss of Jerusalem, had once more a clear objective; but despite the good generalship of Richard I of England, the old fire was lacking. There were endless quarrels among the crusaders, and when Richard at last came within sight of Jerusalem, he obeyed the dictates of strategy, which told him that a siege would be difficult and dangerous, and withdrew. In practical terms it was the right decision; but the crusading movement was at heart a kind of religious fanaticism, and it could achieve its results only if military realities were ignored and the morale of the crusaders kept at fever pitch. The later crusades have few of the stories of miracles and religious exaltation that we find in the First Crusade, and in some measure that is the key to their failure.

There were, of course, other reasons for failure. The Third Crusade did prolong the life of the kingdom of Jerusalem by a century. The Fourth Crusade and its successors, however, went from bad to worse. The Fourth Crusade itself was used to mount an attack on Byzantium and its empire, leading to the installation of a Frankish ruler there and doing irreparable damage to the one other bulwark of Christendom in the East. The Fifth Crusade was aimed at Egypt itself, a tactical decision which was not as extravagant as it seemed: if it had succeeded in taking the Egyptian capital, the effect would have been much the same as that of the attack on Aleppo suggested by Raymond of Antioch on the Second Crusade. Indeed, it was near enough to success for the Egyptians to offer the return of Jerusalem if the crusaders withdrew; but Cardinal Pelagius, the legate in charge of the crusade, refused to negotiate with the infidel, an attitude which underlines the deep distrust (which the crusades had created) between West and East. It was left to the excommunicate Emperor Frederick II to recover the Holy City by diplomacy in 1229; fifteen years later, it was lost again when Turkish horsemen were called in by the Egyptians and took it in the course of a raid on Palestine. All the efforts of subsequent crusades were unable to recover it: St Louis' crusade aimed against Egypt ended in disaster at Damietta in 1250, Edward I's expedition in 1271–2 was too small to be effective. The Frankish lands steadily diminished, and in 1291, with the fall of Acre, the kingdom of Jerusalem came to an end. The survivors fled to Cyprus (captured by Richard I in 1191) and continued to dream of reviving the Christian state in Palestine until the island was in turn taken by the Turks in 1570.

The crusading ideal lingered on, chiefly in the ambitious schemes of religious zealots who hoped to unite the powers of Christendom in one great enterprise. The Hundred Years' War was punctuated by papal appeals for peace on the grounds that England and France ought to unite in a new crusade. As late as 1396, a major expedition was fitted out against the Turks in Hungary. The possible defeat of Bajazet in Bulgaria was no longer seen as even a first step on the road to Jerusalem: the crusade had become simply a war against the infidel. In the event, the impetuosity of the French and Burgundian knights, who attacked the Turkish army when it was drawn up in a carefully prepared defensive position at Nicopolis on the Danube, led to a disaster on the scale of the battle of Hattin, though without equally dire political consequences. Only a handful of the crusaders returned to the West.

Because crusades were idealistic, the product of sudden religious zeal whipped up by preachers, there was always a danger that they would be ill-organised or that would-be crusaders might have second thoughts about their vows. In those respects the world of the military orders was in sharp contrast to that of the crusaders: highly efficient, demanding lifetime commitment from their members, they bore the brunt of the fighting in the kingdom of Jerusalem from the mid-twelfth century onwards. However, just as the crusades broadened in scope and lost their initial impetus, so the military orders changed and broadened with time. The Templars had aroused great enthusiasm in the 1130s, and in 1139 they obtained a papal bull confirming the rule of the order and extending its privileges. Innocent III declared that the order, which was of course already free from secular ties, was to be exempt from all ecclesiastical jurisdiction save that of himself;

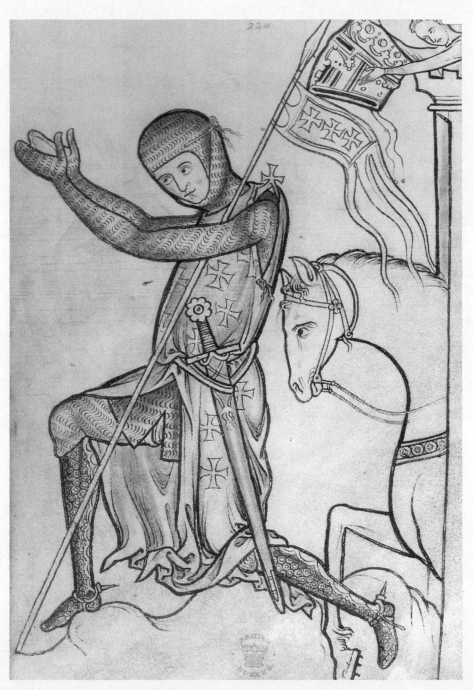

Kneeling crusader by the great thirteenth century artist Matthew Paris

furthermore, like the Cistercians, it was to be exempt from paying tithes. They were therefore virtually a law unto themselves, and as they rapidly became extremely wealthy through pious donations, they came to form a kind of state within a state not only in the kingdom of Jerusalem but also throughout Western Europe. The order was ruled by the Grand Master, but he was only nominally its head. All important decisions had to be discussed by the Grand Chapter, which consisted of the most important officers: only they could sign treaties, declare war, or decide to undertake a siege. The military leader was the Marshal, while administrative matters were the Seneschal's affair. The chief members of the Grand Chapter were the Masters of the various provinces, each province having its own chapter. The organisation was parallel to that of a monastic order, but in political and military affairs such a rigid hierarchy of command was almost unknown. The loose ties of feudal law and the rudimentary discipline of a feudal army were replaced by strict order and discipline, and the order's power over its members was all the more striking because they owed neither secular nor religious allegiance outside its ranks. The code of punishment therefore embraced criminal, religious and disciplinary offences. Only one criminal offence, murder, was punishable by the extreme sanction of expulsion from the order; but a number of disciplinary offences were punishable in this way: treason, desertion, heresy, purchasing entry into the order, plotting among the knights, betrayal of secrets and absence for more than two nights without leave. Anyone expelled under these rules was to be sent to an even stricter order to expiate his sins, though very serious offences were punished by perpetual imprisonment in one of the order's castles.

The Templars therefore had the one element which the ordinary feudal army so conspicuously lacked: a clear cohesion and discipline among their men. They fought for the greater glory of the order, and acts of individual prowess were thus discouraged. At their best, they were superb fighting men, the crack troops of the army of the kingdom of Jerusalem. Yet we hear less in the chronicles of their great victories than of their disasters. Perhaps this is because no Templar chronicles survive, if indeed they were ever written. But even a well-organised fighting force is no better than its leaders; and the leaders had no better appreciation of tactics and strategy than their secular counterparts. Furthermore, the Templars soon realised that their independence from secular ties meant that they could pursue their own course in diplomacy, and they often went against the policy of the kings of

Jerusalem, even though the Grand Master was a member of the kingdom's council or High Court. In 1158 they refused to join an expedition against Egypt, and in 1172 deliberately prevented a proposed alliance between King Amalric and the fanatical members of the Assassin sect. The Assassins, a heretical Islamic sect, eliminated their opponents by murdering them, and in 1173 they were more concerned with settling scores with their Islamic rivals than with the fight against the Christians. They might have been invaluable allies, as Nur-ed-Din was their sworn enemy. But the Templars, annoyed that taxes imposed by them on Assassin villages were to be lifted, and invoking the cry of 'No negotiations with the infidel!', ambushed the Assassin ambassadors and killed them all. The Grand Master refused to hand over the culprits, but Amalric seized them and imprisoned them, thus saving something of the Assassins' goodwill by assuring them that justice had been done. One chronicler says that Amalric was so furious that he threatened to ask the Pope to dissolve the order.

The same indifference to wider considerations and concern for the order's own interests was all too often evident in the order's behaviour in the field. The knights prided themselves by the 1150s on waging an aggressive rather than defensive war against the Moslems, and behaved accordingly. Even though this usually involved little more than border skirmishes, because the knights alone were not numerous enough to mount a campaign, their activities could lead to difficulties when the king was trying to maintain peaceful relations with his neighbours. The desire for glory for the order could create problems as well: at worst, it could lead to organised indiscipline, as serious in its effect as the lack of restraint by feudal cavalry eager for glory on the battlefield. At Ascalon in 1153, when the great sea-fortress was under siege, an accident produced an unexpected breach in the walls in the sector which was the Templars' responsibility. Anxious to reserve the glory for themselves, they posted knights to prevent the rest of the army entering the breach, and sent in forty knights, who were annihilated. The siege was almost abandoned as a result.

Far more serious in its consequences was the conduct of the Templars in the campaign of July 1187. King Guy had assembled an immense army to counter an invasion from Egypt led by Saladin himself, and it was marching to relieve the castle of Tiberias, held by the Countess of Tripoli. It was encamped some eighteen miles from Tiberias, the other side of a strip of barren hills, and in a good defensive position, when messengers came from the castle, asking for immediate help. Many of King Guy's council were eager to move on, anxious to respond chivalrously to the Countess' plight. But Count Raymond of Tripoli, who knew the lie of the land, said that although it was his castle, defended by his wife, that was at stake, he would rather lose both than see the kingdom lost. The council accepted his advice; but that night the Grand Master, Gerard de Ridfort, in his eagerness to attack the enemy, went to King Guy and persuaded him to countermand the council's decision, saying that Raymond was a traitor who, until earlier that year, had made his own truce with Saladin. Guy was swayed, and the army advanced, only to be checked at the crest of the ridge, known as the Horns of Hattin, without water or supplies. The next day Saladin's attack overwhelmed the army; the Templars who survived were captured except for two or three, and Saladin ordered his own equivalent of the Military orders, the Sufis, to slaughter them, excepting only the Grand Master.

Until Hattin, the Templars had been more akin to the men of the First Crusade, fired by an absolutist religious zeal, than to their fellow lords in the kingdom of Jerusalem who, as Sir Steven Runciman says in his great *History of the Crusades*, 'by temperament and from policy were ready to become part of the Oriental world, but were forced by the fanaticism of their newly-come western cousins to take sides'. Indeed, one lord, Reynald of Sidon, on learning of Saladin's triumph, went to him and offered to surrender his castle. He charmed Saladin by his conversation, for he was well versed in Arabic literature, and even gave the impression that he might become a Moslem. In fact, he used the truce which he gained to strengthen his defences, and Saladin was unable to take the castle: but the episode none the less shows how far the Frankish lords had become natives of the East.

In the years following Hattin, this was to be almost equally true of the Templars. In January 1192, the new Grand Master of the Temple advised Richard I not to press home his attack on Jerusalem, but to take the cautious way out and retreat. This policy was repeated in 1219, when the Grand Master opposed a peace treaty with Egypt which included the return of Jerusalem on the grounds that the Holy City could never be held with the resources available. In 1229, when Frederick II obtained its return, the Grand Master refused to recognise the treaty. But this strategic wisdom was not matched by an impeccable regard for the good of the kingdom. An increasing rivalry between the Templars and the Hospitallers, dating back to the late twelfth century, dominated their conduct in the 1240s. For many years the more hot-blooded brethren would draw their swords when they saw a member of the rival order in the streets; in 1242 they were fighting openly in Acre, and throughout the 1240s they deliberately tried to undermine each other's diplomatic efforts, making alliances with different Moslem princes, and in general behaving more like unruly barons than responsible leaders. In 1282, in the dying days of the kingdom, the order was involved in a civil war with the Count of Tripoli.

Part of the order's difficulty was that by 1200 it had grown immensely wealthy. Its European provinces held vast areas of land, and it was one of the largest owners of estates in the kingdom of Jerusalem itself. The need to administer this empire meant that the order needed to recruit clerks rather than knights, and all too often the lands which were meant to finance the Templars' efforts in the Holy Land occupied the order's entire attention. As the years went on, its need for resources grew greater, particularly as it acquired many new possessions from local lords in difficult times, when the latter preferred to sell out and hand over their responsibilities to the order. But as the huge sums of money raised in Europe vanished Eastwards without producing the least result, officers of the order in the West grew less and less inclined to waste the order's resources. Because the order was international, it had become banker to European merchants: sums of money paid in at one commandery could be drawn by a letter addressed to a distant house, thus saving the traveller from carrying gold with him. As the banking system developed, so the order's funds were increasingly committed to it, and less available for use in the East.

But money alone would not have saved the kingdom of Jerusalem. The members of the order no longer had the high morale of their predecessors; mercenaries were hired, not merely to assist the knights, but to carry out many of their functions. In the West, Templars abandoned their frugal ways – Matthew Paris in the 1220s had represented them in the margin of his History of the English riding two to a horse – and instead maintained retinues and wore rich robes. Only in the last days of the kingdom, at the fall of Acre in May 1291, did the order show some of its old high courage. When on 18 May, the rest of the town was taken, the Templars who remained in the town held out in their great tower under their Marshal, and resisted for a further ten days, until Moslem troops swarmed into the collapsing building; the weight of the attackers brought down the whole tower, killing both defenders and attackers.

From Acre, the surviving Templars fled to Cyprus; they also held the little island of Ruad off the Syrian coast for another twelve years. But lack of purpose and the general inclination to blame the military orders for the loss of Palestine undermined what little morale remained. Once again, the Grand Master became involved in political intrigue, meddling in the affairs of Cyprus, while discontent with the order in the West grew year by year. Unlike the Hospitallers, who always maintained charitable establishments and cared for the sick, the Templars were now without a function, and like all medieval bankers, were unpopular by reason of their financial activities.

There were, indeed, schemes afoot for a new shaping of the order. Both Pierre Dubois, who published his pamphlet *On the Recovery of the Holy Land* in 1300, and Ramon Llull, whose scheme appeared in 1305, agreed that the only useful way forward was to unite the two great orders, and the Pope, Clement V, seriously considered this scheme; the Grand Master of the Hospitallers, Fulk de Villaret, was to be head of the new combined 'Knights of Jerusalem'. But the members of the orders had not forgotten the feuds of the previous century and steadfastly refused to have anything to do with the scheme. They were suspicious of the French King, Philip the Fair, who had proposed to the Pope that the kings of France should become the hereditary masters of the orders and that surplus revenues should be at his disposal: but union would have been better for the Templars than the fate which eventually overtook them.

Philip, despite his considerable influence over the papacy, which in 1305 was transferred to Avignon, failed to get his proposal through; so he attacked the Templars on different grounds. Guillaume de Nogaret, his chancellor, had used skilful propaganda based on accusations of heresy against Philip's enemies, and had almost always been successful in obtaining convictions. His own parents had been burnt as Albigensian heretics, and he clearly knew a great deal about heresy trials: he now made accusations against the Templars which were carefully based on earlier cases, notably the charges made against a group of German heretics in 1233. But he may not have acted entirely without foundation: it appears that the star witness in the case, a renegade Templar prior named Esquiu de Floyrian, first made his charges at the court of Jaime II of Aragon. He was clearly an untrustworthy character, and found no audience there, but when he reached France, either Philip or de Nogaret realised the possibilities. But what was Philip's real motive for these attacks? It seems most probable that the wealth of the order was his prime objective;

the Templars were not an important political force in the kingdom, and there is no reason to think that Philip had any personal reasons for disliking them. It may be that he owed them considerable sums, and that they had acted as his bankers: in the light of his own dealings (and those of Edward I and Edward III of England) with Italian bankers, Philip might easily have been heavily in debt to them, but the French financial records of the period are fragmentary, and there is no evidence either way.

Charges based on Esquiu de Floyrian's evidence (suitably embroidered by de Nogaret, one suspects) were first laid before the Pope, Clement V, in 1305, but were not really pressed until the spring of 1307, after the Grand Master of the Temple had arrived in France to discuss the union of the two great military orders, and had indicated his refusal to co-operate. In August 1307, Clement agreed to hold an inquiry, hoping to play for time. Philip was not going to let the Templars prepare their answer. In mid-September secret orders were sent out for the seizure of all Templars and their property on 13 October. The plan worked with incredible smoothness: only thirteen Templars escaped, and the vast majority found themselves in Philip's royal prisons, charged with a variety of crimes. These were primarily concerned with the admission ceremony which, as it was a meeting of the chapter, was held in private. At this ceremony, the new knight was said to have had to deny Christ three times, to spit on a crucifix and to give obscene kisses to the officer admitting him, before worshipping an idol. He was also told that knights were not to refuse to sleep with each other. In the initial shock and confusion, most of the knights, including the Grand Master, Jacques de Molay, admitted some or all of the charges, if only to avoid torture, expecting to be able to retract their oaths later, as being extracted under duress. It was a fatal mistake. Philip had the evidence he needed, and did everything he could to prevent the knights from getting an opportunity to deny the charges in public. Clement V seems to have been convinced that there was indeed something amiss by the readiness with which the knights confessed; his weak resolve and lack of effective power were already handicap enough, and he was not likely to quarrel with Philip, his political master, over an issue in which he was by no means sure of the innocence of Philip's victims.

Philip had none the less acted high-handedly, and the order had many friends outside France. On 22 November Clement did issue a bull ordering other princes to arrest the Templars, but he also ordered the French Templars to be handed over to papal commissioners. Philip could not refuse; once safely out of his clutches, they retracted their confessions to a man. However, the charges had to be dealt with, and in 1309, after much further propaganda had been put out by Philip, the trials began. Philip succeeded in getting his minion, the Archbishop of Sens, put in charge of the proceedings; when the Templars denied the truth of their confessions in court, he declared them to be relapsed heretics, and had fifty-four of them burnt at the stake without further ado. This, and the Grand Master's refusal to undertake the defence of the order (on the reasonable grounds that he could not write, and had no secretaries to help him) demoralised the order, but a defence was organised when the General Council of the Church met at Vienne on the Rhône in the autumn of 1311. However, Philip had put renewed pressure on Clement, and when a handful of the remaining knights appeared at the Council, the Pope adjourned proceedings.

In April the following year, the Council were presented with a bull, *Vox in excelso*, which took the matter out of their hands and settled the order's fate. Clement had issued this at the end of March 'in private consistory', that is, with the help of his personal advisers. He could not condemn the order outright on the evidence produced by Philip, but he was not satisfied that the order was innocent. So he suppressed the order: 'since we cannot do it by law in the light of the inquisition already held, we have effected it by way of a provision or Apostolic order, a sanction against which there is no appeal and which is perpetually valid.' The possessions of the order were to go to the Hospitallers; its chief officers were condemned to perpetual imprisonment at Paris, though the Grand Master and one of his colleagues protested and were promptly burnt by Philip's executioners. Philip likewise flouted the Pope's instructions over the order's possessions: the bulk of these remained in his hands.

Outside France, the knights had fared much better. In England, Aragon and Cyprus, commissions were duly set up to try such Templars as could be arrested, and they were found innocent in almost every case, although a few admitted to spitting on the Cross. This odd blasphemy may have originated in some kind of ritual test of the absolute obedience owed by each knight to his superiors in the order; it was certainly the most frequently admitted item in the catalogue of charges. But apart from this little was done. However, once the papal bull was issued, resistance was useless: the Pope was the supreme head of the order, and his decree could not be flouted. In England Edward II appropriated much of the Templar property, though the Hospitallers gradually won it back: it took them over twenty-five years to obtain possession of the Temple in London. In Aragon, a new order, that of Montesa, was founded, and only the balance of the Templar lands went to the Hospitallers. In Portugal, King Dinis merely refounded the order as the Knights of Christ. The Hospitallers probably benefited most in Germany, where the Templars had been virtually unmolested throughout the period of the trials. The union of the two orders had taken place, but in the least satisfactory way possible.

Why, if they were largely innocent, did an organisation whose spiritual goals and material wealth were so great, succumb to mere propaganda? There are, perhaps, three reasons. First, some of the charges may have had a grain of truth in them, as there are hints of problems with heresy earlier in the order's history – in which case Philip's advisers may have deliberately touched on a sore point, making a defence that much more difficult. But this was the least of the causes. The second reason was undoubtedly the order's wealth, which aroused Philip's greed, and which, as we have seen, tarnished the image of the order in the eyes of those who had once supported it. The sight of Templars living in splendour in the West, instead of fighting in the East, as well as their banking activities, made them unpopular: rumours among the common folk in France vastly exaggerated their crimes, showing how little they were respected. The third and crucial factor, however, was the loss of Palestine. The order was demoralised by this; it had lost many of its best and bravest knights in the fall of Acre, and it no longer had a clear purpose. Furthermore, the Christian West was stunned and bewildered by the disaster: why had the great orders been unable to hold Palestine? A scapegoat was needed, if only to absolve the West from its failure to send effective help. Once the Templars were accused, their crimes became the reason for God's wrath and their failure. With such corruption among its defenders, nothing that other Christians might have done could have saved the Holy Land: such was the implication.

Despite the fall of the Templars, the military orders survived. The idea of a military order had been copied not only by the Hospitallers, but by the Teutonic Knights and by a multiplicity of orders in Spain and Portugal. The Hospitallers were the largest of the remaining orders, and the addition of the Templars' possessions made them even more dominant. Their history in Palestine had in many ways run parallel to that of the Templars, who were both rivals and fellow-warriors. The Hospitallers had begun as a purely charitable order, without military connections, and even after the knights came to dominate the order's activities, they continued to maintain hospitals, and indeed their charitable institutions spread to the West. Whereas a Templar commandery was run entirely for the order's benefit, either as estate or as a rudimentary bank, the Hospitallers looked after the poor and the sick of the neighbourhood, and therefore enjoyed much greater popular support. The Hospitallers had behaved little better than the Templars at many of the critical moments in the history of the kingdom of Jerusalem, though they were perhaps less aggressive in their approach to warfare against the Moslems; but this popular interest in their continuance in the West (because of their hospitals) saved them from the same fate as the Templars. Furthermore, the Templars did little to find a new objective after the fall of Acre, while the energetic Hospitaller leaders had already mapped out their new role by 1307.

Both orders had maintained small fleets for naval warfare and for transport but these had been relatively unimportant while they held castles in Palestine itself. The Hospitallers, however, realised that any future war against the Moslems and any possible expedition to recover the Holy Land would have to be sea-borne, and as early as 1299 their admiral was promoted to the inner council of the order. They also realised that it would be a mistake to keep their headquarters in Cyprus, where it was difficult to avoid involvement in royal politics, and where their possessions were not extensive. In 1307 they had taken Rhodes, largely because the pirates who infested the island were disrupting Christian trade in the East, and in 1310 Fulk de Villaret, the Grand Master, transferred the order's headquarters to Rhodes, a far-sighted move which meant that the order became an independent sovereign state. The example of the Teutonic knights, who had established themselves on a similar basis in Prussia, may have played some part in his decision. But this achievement was not attained without difficulty. De Villaret was an autocratic personality, and in an order which was run on democratic lines, this made him unpopular. A rival master was elected in 1317 but in 1319 he was forced to resign.

Quarrels of this kind continued throughout the fourteenth century, partly a symptom of the difficulties caused by the disappearance of the order's main function as defender of Palestine, partly due to the problems of adjustment to a situation where the order was very wealthy, attracting able men, yet unable to give them much scope for activity. A great chapter-general in 1331 at Montpellier and subsequent reforms down to 1370 saved the order from permanent harm. In particular, division into *langues*, by which the knights were grouped by their country of origin and each *langue* was given a particular post to guarantee a balance of power, stood the order in good stead in a period when national feeling was increasing in Europe, and national rivalries could easily have led to grave disturbances inside the order.

If the fourteenth century was mainly a period of consolidation for the knights of the orders, it was also punctuated by attempts to revive the attack on the Moslems. These expeditions, although dignified by the name of crusade, were really part of a long struggle for control of the eastern Mediterranean. In 1345 Smyrna was taken and a fleet intended for the invasion of Rhodes was destroyed. This was followed by a French expedition in 1346–7, and a Cypriot crusade in 1365. The latter, led by the King of Cyprus Pierre I de Lusignan, only succeeded in adding another black episode to the history of the 'holy wars': the sack of Alexandria, the slaughter of its inhabitants and the destruction of its priceless library of ancient manuscripts. The booty was such that the majority of the crusaders refused to continue and sailed back to Cyprus. What was needed was not simply military zeal but discipline and a real commitment to the crusade. Philippe de Mézières, who was chancellor to Pierre I at the time of the crusade, and who was present at Alexandria, put the ideas produced by his experience into yet another scheme for a new crusade. *The Dream of the Old Pilgrim*, as he called his work, is one of the best argued plans for the reconquest of the East, but in the end it only shows how impossible the vision of a holy war had become. It was no longer a matter of raising an army but, so de Mézières felt, a question of reforming society in the West so that the Christian world would approach such an enterprise in the right spirit. He would have been appalled by the crusade of 1396 which ended in disaster at Nicopolis, undertaken in exactly the spirit of chivalric bravado he had come to deplore.

The Hospitallers, meanwhile, did what they could against the encroaching might of the Moslem world. With Byzantium barely able to defend itself and the Turks established not only throughout Asia Minor but in much of south-east Europe, the balance of power was now very much in the Moslems' favour; but the crusaders themselves were largely to blame for the collapse of the one inherently friendly power in the East, because the decline of Byzantine power was virtually a direct result of the Fourth Crusade. In this hostile environment, the Hospitallers could do little: grandiose schemes for the establishment of a state in southern Greece came to nothing, and their chief activity became raids on Moslem shipping and on the coastal towns.

They were sufficiently successful to provoke counter-attacks, especially since after the conquest of Cyprus in 1426, that kingdom was a Christian vassal-state of the sultans of Egypt and took no further part in the campaigns against the Moslems. In 1435, Sultan Baybars planned to attack Rhodes, and re-inforcements were hurriedly brought in from the West. But it was not until 1444 that the invasion took place, and the town of Rhodes was besieged for a month until a bold sortie destroyed the Egyptian camp and put the invaders to flight.

With the fall of Constantinople in 1453, the Knights of St John were the only remaining Christian power in the East, and the Ottoman Turks soon turned their attention to reducing this last outpost, at first demanding tribute, and then negotiating a series of uneasy truces. In 1480, Mahomet II, the conqueror of Byzantium, determined to deal with Rhodes. Palaeologos Pasha, a Greek in Mahomet's service, was sent to capture the island with a huge force, rumoured to be seventy thousand strong. Against this vast horde the knights could muster perhaps two thousand men-at-arms, but the Grand Master, D'Aubusson, had been making preparations for the expected invasion for almost a year. One of the defenders wrote before the siege: 'The city is well provided with grain, wine, oil, cheese, salted meat and other foodstuffs ... many crossbows and both heavy and light guns and earthenware fire-pots and receptacles for boiling oil and Greek fire and pots full of pitch lashed together ... and there is a continuous watch by day and night of select companies of crossbowmen and handgunners and a hundred cavalry.' This was not to be a medieval siege, fought with stone-throwing machines, siege towers, scaling ladders and mines, where the skirmishes would be hand-to-hand and individual bravery would count for much: rather, it was one of the first great duels of bombardment and counter-bombardment, in which the skill of gunners and engineers predominated. When the Turks landed on 23 May 1480, their first action was to site a heavy artillery battery, capable of firing huge cannonballs three feet in diameter, outside the walls.

The Turks concentrated their attack on the mole which protected the harbour, defended by a massive tower; but although they reduced the tower to rubble within a few days, the knights improvised defences out of its ruins and repulsed a major attack on it early in June. This unexpectedly steadfast opposition led the Turks to open another area of attack, on the northern walls of the town, and soon the town itself was under heavy bombardment. Well-organised precautions ensured that casualties were light, and morale among the knights remained high. A renewed assault on the harbour tower on 18 June at night was driven off with heavy losses, thanks to the personal intervention of the Grand Master, but by now the stresses of the siege were beginning to tell, and some knights began to favour surrender. D'Aubusson told them that 'since they were in such terror of Mahomet they might leave at once, and he would personally cover their retreat; but if they remained there must be no more talk of surrender.' The knights, duly abashed, begged to be allowed to redeem their honour in action.

The Turkish artillery had breached the wall to the north of the city, but new defences had been put up within the city. None the less, when the Turks launched an attack on 27 July, they were able to seize a ruined tower on the outer wall, and the situation looked very dangerous. Once again, D'Aubusson's own presence of mind saved the situation, for he blocked the walkway leading from the tower on to the other walls and held it until his men were able to recapture the tower and drive off the attackers with heavy losses. The Turks were exhausted, and Palaeologos Pasha gave the order to strike camp. On 7 August all the besiegers had left. Almost half the knights had been killed, and much of the city ruined; but their courage had succeeded in overcoming the best artillery and one of the largest armies of the day.

The order had won a respite, but in the face of growing Turkish power it was no more than a respite. D'Aubusson, who recovered from the serious wounds he received during the siege and continued as Grand Master until 1503, was fully aware of this, and devoted his energies to restoring the town's defences and recruiting new knights. The rebuilding was directed by the finest engineers of the time, and made Rhodes one of the best-fortified towns in the Christian world. Meanwhile, the naval warfare against the Turks continued, culminating in a great victory off Alexandretta in 1510 when de L'Isle Adam, commanding the order's fleet, captured the larger part of a Mameluke fleet. But it was the last triumph: for the Turks, in the course of the next decade, destroyed the Mamelukes, seized Egypt and emerged as sole masters of Islam. Once again the knights prepared for a siege, and yet more fortifications were built.

When the moment came, it was de L'Isle Adam, elected Master in 1521, who was in command. His opponent was the sultan Suleiman, later known as Suleiman the Magnificent. De L'Isle Adam knew that he could expect little help from the West, torn by religious and political divisions, and the Turkish resources were now greater than ever. He organised the defence of the town with the greatest care, leaving nothing to chance, and provisioned it for a year's siege. When the Turks arrived, in late June 1522, they faced a small but determined force, not much larger than that which had held the town in 1480. Their own army was perhaps twice as numerous as that of 1480, commanded by Suleiman's Grand Vizier, Pir Mahomet Pasha.

In the light of their experiences in 1480, the Turks wasted little time on the harbour tower, but concentrated instead on making a great breach in the walls in the sector defended by the knights of England and Aragon. Mines and countermines, the latter directed by the order's engineer, Tadim, who was made an honorary knight, were dug. For the first month of the siege proper, from late July to late August, much of the activity was underground, and as much as five-sixths of the outer wall had been tunnelled under, with Tadim's countermines cutting across Turkish tunnels. But despite his precautions a mine was set off under the bastion of England on 4 September, producing a breach twelve yards wide in the wall. From now on there were almost daily assaults on one section of the wall or another, and even though the knights' losses were disproportionately small, they were very serious because there was no hope of reinforcement, while the Turkish army had no such problem. On 24 September a general assault was ordered, the brunt of it taken by the bastion of Aragon. An heroic resistance held the great breaches in the wall against the sultan's picked troops, and the cannon of the knights mowed down the attackers: after a few hours, the Turks were beaten off.

However, the knights had lost yet more men, and morale was declining. In late October, the Chancellor of the order was implicated in a plot to surrender the town; he was found guilty, on dubious evidence, and executed. A few reinforcements did reach the town, and the lack of activity from the Turks indicated that they were finding conditions in their camp difficult. Early in December, a succession of messengers offering peace terms appeared outside the walls, and de L'Isle Adam, despite his own wish to fight to the bitter end, summoned the council to consider accepting terms, if only because of the citizens of the town. On 11 December terms were agreed: the knights could leave in peace, as well as any citizens who wished to follow them, and lives and property would be respected. But the citizens were not happy about the guarantees, and the truce was briefly broken before peace was finally made. On 26 December de L'Isle Adam went to ratify the treaty: Suleiman is reported to have said to his Grand Vizier as he left: 'It saddens me to have to drive this brave old man from his home.' The next day Suleiman came into

Rhodes; as he entered, he dismissed his guard, saying: 'My safety is guaranteed by the words of a Grand Master of the Hospitallers, which is more sure than all the armies in the world.' It was a fitting tribute to the knights and their leader: in an age of scepticism and corruption in the Church, they had provided an example of outstanding faith and courage. In the words of the Emperor Charles V, one of the monarchs who had failed to send help, 'nothing in the world was so well lost as Rhodes'.

Charles V was to provide the order with its next home after seven years of wandering. The Emperor was persuaded to grant to the knights Malta and Tripoli, outlying possessions of his far-flung empire which were strategically important but which he was unable to exploit with his thinly-spread military resources. Here de L'Isle Adam re-established the order as a military power. Lacking the resources of Rhodes, a rich and fertile island, on barren Malta the knights became raiders against the Moslems not only for the cause of the faith but also from economic necessity. Though they lost Tripoli in 1551, they conducted expeditions against the corsair bases in North Africa with considerable success, and their reputation for seamanship and ferocious fighting ability grew with the years. In 1564, for example, they seized a great galley bound for Constantinople far off in the Greek Islands and towed it back to Malta, with a cargo valued at 80,000 ducats. This exploit and others of the same kind determined Suleiman, now aged seventy, to renew his attack on the order. In the spring of 1565, forty-two years after he had forced them to leave Rhodes, his war-fleet sailed once more against the knights.

The knights had built a new citadel on the island overlooking the best of the two large natural harbours on the island, and had fortified the whole of this inlet, known as Grand Harbour. The Grand Master, La Valette, had spent great sums on these defences since his election in 1557, and had revitalised the whole order; when he heard of Suleiman's plans, he at once summoned all the available knights. There were not many more than there had been at Rhodes, perhaps seven hundred at most, but there were probably more auxiliary troops. The island was well-provisioned, though not as well as La Valette would have liked, and supplies were used sparingly even before the siege began.

The first Turkish ships were sighted on 18 May, and within a few days the whole force had landed, some thirty to forty thousand strong. They found the countryside deserted with all available food gathered into the fortresses. Their commanders, Mustafa Pasha and the Admiral Piali, landed unopposed with their men; La Valette knew that he could not meet such a host in the open field. He had poisoned all the wells in the countryside, and was fully aware that his best hope was to prolong the siege until the discomforts of a siege camp on a barren island began to take their toll. The tactics of the siege itself were to be different from the attack on Rhodes. The fortifications at Rhodes were built on soft ground, which could be mined. Those at Malta were founded on rock, so artillery became all-important. The Turkish artillery was even more formidable than it had been in 1522, and within days of the landing the great guns were pounding away at the key fort of St Elmo, at the mouth of Grand Harbour. But until St Elmo was reduced, no attack on the main fortress, to the south of the inlet, was possible.

St Elmo had been fortified with the utmost care, and it was difficult for the Turkish guns to get within range at first, but within days they had made life in the fort, which had no underground passageways for communications, almost intolerable. La Valette had to send for precious reserves before the end of May, and on 3 June some of the outworks were taken by the Turks. A general assault on the fort followed, but here La Valette's preparations turned the tide. The fort was stocked with every kind of 'anti-personnel device', including Greek fire and blazing wooden hoops steeped in specially prepared incendiary mixtures, and with the help of these the defenders decimated the Turks, whose flowing robes made them an easy prey to such weapons; furthermore, it was the crack Turkish troops, the Janissaries, who suffered the greatest losses. A further great assault was made on 10 June, yet the defenders still managed to drive off the oncoming hordes, and again on 16 June the fort held out against all the odds. In the following days one of the three generals commanding the Turks, the experienced corsair Dragut, was mortally wounded, as well as another senior officer. St Elmo had been expected to hold out for a fortnight; it had already lasted for a month, and still the mere handful of knights resisted. But their courage was not enough against such overwhelming odds, and on 23 June, the survivors, including the wounded sitting in chairs to man the ramparts, were killed to a man.

A brief respite followed while the Turkish engineers moved their artillery positions to concentrate on the fort of Sant' Angelo; but they realised this was impossible, and decided instead to try to gain a foothold on the peninsula to the south of the citadel. La Valette threw up an improvised palisade, but the Turks attacked early in July. Only an heroic defence held them back, and the tide was turned when a concealed battery destroyed ten boat-loads of

The Knight and Society

Chivalry is the interface between the knight's military function and his role in society; at court he might be a member of a knightly order, in church he might be a devotee of St George, and in his love life he might follow the ideas of courtly love. The rituals of knighthood and its prestige were an important part of chivalry, while tournaments, fought under the admiring gaze of ladies and followed by dancing, were the high points of a knight's social calendar.

The knight at the magic fountain at dawn: a scene from René d'Anjou's allegorical romance
The Book of the Heart captured by Love

ROMANCES

(right) *The round table from Winchester Castle: a recreation of king Arthur's round table, probably made for Edward III and repainted for Henry VIII*

(below) *The appearance of the Grail at king Arthur's court: the legend of the Grail, uniting the religious and secular aspects of chivalry, was the greatest of all the romances*

KNIGHTS AND LADIES

(above) *Miniature of the troubadour, Bernart de Ventadorn*

(left) *Ulrich von Lichtenstein,* minnesänger *and author of a highly romantic autobiography,* The Service of Ladies

(below left) *Duke John of Brabant, who was killed in a tournament in 1294*

(below right) *Heinrich von Breslau receives the victor's wreath from his lady*

KNIGHTS
AND LADIES

(opposite and left) *A joust with ladies watching behind barriers, and the dancing after the event, from the fourteenth century manuscript of Jacques Bretel's* The Tournament at Chauvency

(below) *A dramatic mêlée: an Italian tournament of the fourteenth century with a gallery of ladies looking on*

THE RITUALS AND
BELIEFS OF KNIGHTHOOD

(opposite) *The statutes of the Order of the Holy Ghost, showing the annual gathering of the knights of the order; a member who has transgressed the rules is shown eating alone in penitent costume at the feast*

(right) *The making of a knight: the girding on of swords*

(below) *Sir Geoffrey Luttrell departing for war or jousting, taking leave of his wife and daughter*

The story of St George, the patron saint of knighthood, from a book made in Paris for the duke of Bedford in 1424-5

Janissaries coming up as reinforcements at a single broadside. Even so, the Turkish attacks were now directed at the outworks of the main citadel itself, the forts which guarded the dockyard creek and the landward wall, or bastion of Castile. On 2 August, after a fortnight of bombardment, the first direct assault came, preceded by gunfire so intense that it could be heard seventy miles away in Sicily. It lasted for six hours, but the knights, even though their massive defences began to crumble under the gunfire, were able to repel the attack. Five days later, after almost continuous bombardment, another assault was launched. It was a two-pronged attack, but one of the onslaughts was checked by the layout of the defences, and thousands of Turks were trapped and massacred between the inner and outer walls. The other attack very nearly succeeded, but word came to the Turkish commander that his camp had been sacked; assuming that fresh troops must have landed to relieve the besiegers, he called off his men, only to find that the havoc had been wrought by a cavalry force from Mdina, where a handful of the knights still held the old citadel. For the moment the knights were saved.

The next Turkish attack was a combination of artillery bombardment and mining. Their engineers had found that it was possible, though very difficult, to mine the landward wall of the citadel, and by 18 August this section of the defences, the bastion of Castile, had been undermined. That day a feint attack was made on the seaward side, but La Valette was not daunted by this, and even though a great breach was made when the mine was exploded, the Turks were unable to gain more than a brief foothold inside the walls. But the breach was serious, and a siege tower was also against the walls, serving as a possible access point for an attack. La Valette ordered the wall opposite the siege tower to be opened, and demolished its base with cannon fire. Another attempt to make a breach in the walls with a slow fuse bomb was thwarted when the knights threw it back among the Turks, where it caused great damage. These blows to Turkish morale were accompanied by sickness in their camp and quarrels between their two remaining commanders; but the situation of the defenders was little better, with the outworks of the citadel in ruins.

However, the knights had supplied their garrisons for a very long siege, and at no point did their supplies fail. The Turks, on the other hand, had expected the siege to be relatively short, and were now beginning to run short of powder, while food supplies were low and their supply ships were being intercepted by Christian corsairs. In a desperate attempt to gain supplies they marched on Mdina, but the governor dressed all the inhabitants as men-at-arms and paraded them on the ramparts; Mdina's defences were strong, and the prospect of attacking troops who were fresh and well-ensconced was too much for both the Turkish soldiers and their commander. A new complication now arose, in that the joint commander responsible for the fleet, Piali, insisted that he must withdraw his ships before the autumn winds made it dangerous to risk the thousand-mile voyage home. Once again, on 1 September, a general assault was made, but it was driven off with relative ease. It was to be the last attack: on 7 September a relief force commanded by the viceroy of Sicily landed, and the Turkish commanders at once ordered their troops to embark. But when he learnt how small the relief force was the commander of the army ordered his troops to return ashore. It was too late: faced by troops in good spirit and condition, the best of the Turkish army was soon routed. The knights had defeated the full might of Islam.

It was to be their last great encounter with the Moslems. Turkish sea-power was crushed at Lepanto six years later, and Malta itself was turned into a masterpiece of military engineering. A new citadel, named Valetta after the heroic Grand Master, was raised on the northern shore of the harbour, incorporating all the improvements suggested by the experience of the siege. But Moslem power was in decline, and although the knights fought in Eastern Europe and Crete for another century, and there were occasional skirmishes at sea well into the eighteenth century, the disappearance of their enemy and the deep changes in the Christian West made them a proud relic of the past. When Napoleon came to Malta in 1798, they resisted for only two days before surrendering to the new infidels.

The crusades in the eastern Mediterranean ended in failure; the wars against the Moslems at the other end of that sea ended in success, though over a longer period. The Spanish Reconquista was from the start more of a political war than the fighting in Palestine had ever been, but it too had its moments when chivalry and religion merged. In 1063, an expedition was organised in France to go to the relief of Barbastro, on the southern slopes of the Pyrenees; it had the blessing of the Pope, and was in some ways a kind of forerunner of the First Crusade – though the soldiers involved were more interested in booty and the pleasures of the conquered harems than in any high religious goal. There were no holy places to be fought for in Spain; only the wealth of the Arab caliphate of Cordoba, which at one time held sway over half of Islam, was the real lure. Yet because it was a war against the infidel, it did at times become a war fought with religious zeal. The beginnings of the Reconquista centred on the discovery of the body of St James at Compostela, and the town became, like Jerusalem, a great centre of pilgrimage. Instead of the relics of the Holy Cross, the Spanish armies took as their banner the figure of St James on his white horse, 'Santiago Matamoros', 'St James the slayer of the Moors'.

The idea of the military orders was welcomed even more enthusiastically in Spain than elsewhere in Europe, and from 1130 onwards Templar foundations were common. In 1134 Alfonso the Warrior went so far as to leave his kingdom of Aragon to them and the Hospitallers, but in fact the knights settled for a number of castles. They soon became involved in the frontier wars against the Moslems of southern Spain, but their prime objective

Gift of the castle of Ucles to the Spanish Order of Santiago

in holding lands in Europe was to raise money for Palestine, not to get involved on a new front against the infidels. By 1157 they had decided against using their precious resources in this way, and told Sancho of Castile that they were abandoning their fortress of Calatrava because they expected a Moslem attack and did not have the men to defend it. The King offered it to anyone who would take it, with sufficient lands to support the cost of defending it, but was unable to replace the Templars until a nobleman who had become a Cistercian monk persuaded his abbot, Ramon of Fitero, to accept responsibility for it. Enrolling knights to help him, Ramon held the castle as a kind of fortified monastic community until his death in 1164. The monks then chose a new abbot and withdrew from Calatrava, but the knights, who had adopted a simple form of religious rule, elected a different leader and remained in the castle. The knights were reluctant to abandon their religious connections and applied for a rule modelled on existing religious orders and linked to the Cistercians, who remained as the superior authority over the order.

The prime loyalty of Calatrava's knights was to king and kingdom. At the election of a new master of Calatrava, he swore loyalty to the King of Castile, a significant change from the fierce independence of the Templars and Hospitallers within the kingdom of Jerusalem. The Cistercian influence was really limited to the clergy-brethen rather than to the knights. Its early years were marked by energetic warfare against the Moslems, with varying results; the defeat of the Castilian army at Alarcos in 1195 led to the loss of Calatrava itself, but in 1212 the great victory at Las Navas de Tolosa restored their headquarters to them. They chose, however, to rebuild at a more healthy site nearer the frontier, and Calatrava la Nueva became their permanent home. Here a pattern of frontier settlement based on fortified villages and ranch-style farming developed, which was later to influence Spanish settlements in the New World. But the order's economic and military strength was undermined by political difficulties. By the 1240s, only noble recruits could be admitted: the ties with the royal court were increasingly close, and from the late thirteenth century onwards royal intervention in elections was a matter of course. Calatrava might be wealthy in Spanish terms, but it had none of the international resources and prestige of the Templars and Hospitallers to enable it to resist such political pressures.

Meanwhile, Calatrava's example had been imitated: in the kingdom of León the Order of Alcantara was formed by 1183, but it never became very powerful, and soon sought Calatrava's protection. More important was the foundation of the Order of Santiago in the 1170s. A much later tradition claimed that its origins went back to the dark days of the civil wars of the eleventh century when thirteen knights, horrified at the way in which their fellow-Christians fought each other, vowed never to unsheath their swords against a Christian, and promised to devote themselves to the fight against the heathen. In fact, the order did have a secular origin in that it grew out of a guild brotherhood of knights who had undertaken to protect pilgrims going to Compostela, and its remarkable statutes bear witness to this. It was the only order whose rule was based on that of Augustinian canons rather than an enclosed order: its clergy-brethen were in fact canons, but many of the knight-brothers were married, their families and goods being part of the order. They lived in community in their *encomiendas*, castles or fortified villages; when a married knight died, the order cared for his family, but his property went to the order. The order was also active in redeeming prisoners from the Arabs, and by 1184 had two establishments devoted to this cause.

The great period of the orders was during the thirteenth century under Fernando III of Castile, who brought a crusader's fervour to the war against the Moors. The kingdoms of the south were disunited, while Fernando inherited the throne of León in 1230. In the following decade he took Trujillo and Alcatraz, defeated a Moorish army at Jerez and seized Cordoba itself. His greatest triumph was the siege and capture of Seville in 1247–8: the knights of Santiago were the first to enter the walls. By 1262, only the kingdom of Granada remained, in uneasy alliance with the Christians. But with Fernando's death in 1252 the impetus had gone. The last stages were to take another two hundred years to complete.

The years of relative peace that followed undermined the order's morale. Their wealth was no longer used to equip armies and increasingly the Masters acted like secular princes. Knights were no longer admitted by the prior as religious head of the order, but by the Master himself. Mercenaries were hired to supplement, and in some cases to supplant, the knights in the field. At Alcantara in 1318 a disputed deposition of the Master led to civil war between the knights; likewise, there was fighting among the knights of Calatrava in the 1320s. The suppression of the Templars weakened the prestige of the orders, even though it led to the creation of two new orders, the Knights of Christ in Portugal and the Knights of Montesa in Aragon. However, under Alfonso XI of Castile there was a renewed call to arms, and this burst of activity put new life into the orders, even though Alfonso now disposed of the Masterships without any pretence that the orders were independent. In 1340, the orders gave crucial help to Alfonso in his victory over a Moslem invasion force from North Africa, and they were prominent at the siege and capture of Algeciras in 1344. But with Alfonso's death in 1350, the kingdom passed to his infant son Pedro, and civil war, instead of wars against the Moslems, once again prevailed.

The last half of the fourteenth century was a black period for Castile as well as for the orders. Civil war between Pedro 'the Cruel' and his bastard half-brother Enrique of Trastamare broke out in 1365; Pedro was driven from his throne, but enlisted the aid of the Black Prince. At the Battle of Najera in 1367 members of the orders fought on both sides, though two of the Grand Masters were in Enrique's army; the Black Prince's men captured them after the battle, the Grand Master of Calatrava being found in a cellar in the town of Najera and the Grand Master of Santiago hiding behind a high wall with the prior of the Hospitallers. Other Grand Masters met violent ends: between 1355 and 1371, six out of sixteen Masters of the three Castilian orders were either murdered or killed in civil wars. The death of Pedro at Enrique's hands in 1369 did not signify the end of the troubles: war between Portugal and Castile broke out in 1385, and when the vastly larger Castilian army was routed at Aljubarrota, the Master of Calatrava was killed. The Portuguese throne passed to the Master of the Knights of Christ, João, and this small order naturally flourished after his accession as king.

The crusading spirit was not dead, however, and in 1394 the Master of Alcantara led an expedition against the kingdom of Granada, but he and his men fell into an ambush in the difficult mountainous terrain and were massacred. This reverse was avenged in 1410, when Antequerra and Almería were taken, and in 1421 Huescar, held by the Moors for seven hundred years, fell to a new crusade. However, the pattern of civil war was not easily broken, and most of the fifteenth-century history of the orders is concerned with internal politics. The orders themselves had become among the wealthiest and most powerful institutions in the kingdom of Castile, and their Mastership was now all too often a purely political appointment, eight-year-olds or married nobles who had never been members of the order being elected by royal decree. Occasionally a suitable candidate did in fact become Master; but the internal dissensions of Castile prevented even the most enthusiastic Master from taking effective action against the Moors.

Meanwhile, the Portuguese knights had begun to imitate the Hospitallers, and had become a largely sea-borne organisation which equipped expeditions against Tangier in 1437 and again in 1463 and 1464, until the town was taken in 1471. Their ships played an active part both in raids on the North African coast and in the exploration of West Africa: the old red cross of the Templars, adopted by the Knights of Christ, was seen in exotic places as the caravels pushed further and further south. But whereas the Hospitallers were mainly concerned to destroy Moslem commerce, the Portuguese navigators, whether from the royal fleet or those of the orders, were engaged in developing trade with the African coastal states rather than carrying out a crusade against them.

The last great figure of the Spanish orders, Rodrigo Téllez Giron, embodies many of the contradictions of the orders in this period. He was the illegitimate son of Pedro Giron, Master of Calatrava, who had renounced his support for Alfonso, rival claimant for the throne to Isabella, on condition that he should marry the latter. He died before the marriage could take place, but he had already resigned his Mastership and installed his son. The order was ruled by four guardians during his minority; however, this was not as harmful as was usually the case, and constructive reforms were carried out. Rodrigo proved to be as energetic a soldier as his father, who had carried out over a dozen major raids on the kingdom of Granada, and with the union of Castile and Aragon under 'the Catholic king' Ferdinand who married Isabella, the renewal of the Reconquista took place in earnest. The defiant attitude of Granada after 1476, including a refusal to pay tribute and the seizure of a frontier town in 1481, provoked a swift reaction. The town of Alhama was taken in 1482, but when Ferdinand attacked Loja later that year, he was ambushed in the mountains, and Rodrigo was killed in the ensuing battle.

It seemed as though Granada would survive for another century, as it had done since the last serious attacks by the Christians, but the Christian kingdoms were united under determined leadership, while the Moors were now the ones to fight over disputed successions. Ferdinand raised a new army, hiring the very latest technicians, German gunners, Swiss pikemen, Italian engineers, instead of relying on the traditional warfare of the orders. The city of Ronda, thought to be impossible to capture because of its situation, fell to the gunners in ten days, reduced to rubble by their barrage, and the Moorish kingdom began to crumble. Málaga, despite its massive defences, fell in 1487; Almería, after withstanding Ferdinand in 1488, was taken in 1489 after a five-month siege. Two years later, in April 1491, Granada itself was besieged.

Despite a fierce resistance – the besiegers' camp was burnt and had to be replaced by a permanent town, the 'Holy City' of Santa Fé – the last Moorish ruler in Spain was forced to surrender. On the morning of 2 January 1492 the acting Master of Calatrava set up a crucifix on the Alhambra and the Grand Master of Santiago unfurled the crimson banner of St James. The work of the Reconquista was over.

This left the orders without a purpose, stranded like sea-monsters after a flood. They were immensely wealthy, indeed far too wealthy and powerful for any king in the Renaissance world to tolerate their existence as independent entities. The Mastership of Calatrava was already in the care of the crown when Granada fell; in 1493 Santiago fell vacant and in the following year the Master of Alcantara resigned. In 1523 these 'provisional' arrangements were made permanent; the senior officials were already royal nominees, and by the mid-sixteenth century the orders had become no more than a secular shadow of their former selves.

The military orders in Palestine and Spain developed as a result of a crusade – in its broadest sense – which already existed. The third great area of activity, in north-east Europe, was actually chosen by a military order as the scene of its activities. The Order of Teutonic Knights had begun as a hospital for the sick and wounded at the siege of Acre in 1190. By 1198, it had followed the pattern of the Hospitallers and had become a military order, though the rule chosen was that of the Templars. This new order had to compete for support with the much more evocative names of Templar and Hospitaller, and its early growth was slow. In 1210, Hermann von Salza, an able diplomat and commander, was elected Grand Master, and his thirty years as head of the order were to prove the turning point. First, although von Salza spent much of his time in the East, whether on crusade with St Louis, or at Frederick II's side when he re-entered Jerusalem in 1229, a new outlet for the order's energies was found when the King of Hungary, and later a Polish duke, enlisted the order's help against the heathen. The idea of a crusade in Eastern Europe was originally suggested by the Hungarian King, but having obtained his immediate objective with the help of the knights, he refused to reward them as promised. None the less, the idea that this was territory suitable for a crusade had been established, and when in 1217 the bishop responsible for missionary activity in Prussia asked for a crusade to protect his new converts, many ordinary knights answered his request. In 1221 the first crusade against the Prussians was launched, but it provoked such a backlash that the Duke of Masovia, on the Prussian border, asked the Teutonic knights for help. They agreed, but on rigorous terms. Anxious to avoid another betrayal such as they had suffered in Hungary, they demanded the whole of Kulmerland from the Duke, to be held from him as overlord, but with all other rights transferred to the order. In 1228 the first castle was built there, at Vogelsang on the Elbe; and with their military and political base secure, the Teutonic knights set out on their first campaign.

The knights' white cloaks with black crosses were to inspire terror in the Prussians for the next two centuries, but the contest was by no means as unequal as it might seem. The knights were equipped for warfare in the West or in Palestine; they learnt only gradually that war against an elusive, fierce race used to hiding in forests and swamps was a very different matter. Again and again a great military effort appeared to have overcome all resistance when the fires of revolt would break out. Even when the land was taken piecemeal, settlements and castles established, and every trace of resistance had appar-

Schloss Marienburg, headquarters of the Teutonic Knights in Prussia

ently vanished, the Prussians would invoke their heathen gods again and massacre the newcomers. Fortunately, the knights based their strategy on strong castles, such as the fortresses at Thorn, Kulm and Marienwerder. In times of trouble they could withdraw into the safety of these, knowing that the Prussians were ignorant of siegecraft, and watch the rebellion flare up and burn itself out like a scrub fire.

By the time of Hermann von Salza's death the knights were firmly established in Prussia, drawing revenues from lands which had been given to them in Germany, and with only slight involvement in Palestine. Prussia, however, was not the only area in Eastern Europe where missionaries were at work: similar conditions prevailed in the Baltic in the area known as Livonia (now Estonia, Latvia and Lithuania). Here a small military order had been founded in the first years of the thirteenth century, the Brethren of the Sword. The Estonians were more formidable opponents than the Prussians, and there were added complications of commercial rivalry and interference by a papal legate at Riga, a rapidly developing port for the trade with Prussia. By 1230 the Brethren of the Sword had opened negotiations for union with the Teutonic order which, because it had absorbed the minute Order of Dobrin, already had interests in the area. Little progress was made, though, before half the army of the Brethren of the Sword was annihilated at Saulen during a foolhardy winter campaign in 1236. Gregory IX now enforced the proposed union.

If all had gone well in Prussia, the Teutonic knights would simply have transferred their efforts northwards; but the Prussian conquest was far from complete. A greater revolt in 1242 led to thirty years of intermittent revolt and repression, in which the order survived only with considerable help from outside. Livonia was a drain on the order's resources during this time, the most serious episode being Alexander Nevsky's defeat of the knights and their army on the frozen Lake Peipus in 1242. This not only established the Russian princes as a substantial power, ruling out the order's dream of expansion eastward, but led to a general revolt in Livonia and helped to spark off that in Prussia. The knights fought back, however, and by 1260 they had linked their two territories by taking the whole of the Baltic coast. But their men were very thinly deployed as a result, and a serious defeat in that year in Samland, the area between Prussia and Livonia, meant that the ensuing rebellion succeeded in breaking the new and fragile link. It took thirty years to repair the damage, but by 1290 the coastal strip was reconquered and the last flickers of revolt had been extinguished.

The lands which the order held at the beginning of the fourteenth century were to form the basis of its later strength; but the campaigns against the heathen continued. A new Lithuanian leader appeared in 1310, and during the next seventy years the order's armies set out against the pagan as often as eight times a year, supported by crusaders from the West. Henry, Earl of Derby, later Earl of Lancaster, was one of these: in 1351, during a lull in the Anglo-French war, he set out for Prussia with a group of other English knights. He, and possibly some of his companions, had been at the siege of Algeciras in 1343, and Chaucer was probably thinking of his campaign when he described the knight in the *Canterbury Tales*, though Chaucer's hero had also seen service in the eastern Mediterranean under Pierre de Lusignan:

When we took Alexandria, he was there.
He often sat at table in the chair
Of honour, above all nations, when in Prussia.
In Lithuania he had ridden, and Russia,
No Christian man so often, of his rank.
When, in Granada, Algeciras sank
Under assault, he had been there, and in
North Africa, raiding Benamarin;
In Anatolia he had been as well
And fought when Ayas and Attalia fell,
For all along the Mediterranean coast
He had embarked with many a noble host.
In fifteen mortal battles he had been
And jousted for our faith at Tramissene
Thrice in the lists, and always killed his man.
This same distinguished knight had led the van
Once with the Bey of Balat, doing work
For him against another heathen Turk;
He was of sovereign value in all eyes.

Fighting in Prussia was regarded as fully on a par with other crusading enterprises, though the hazards were perhaps rather different, and life in the Teutonic knight's castles more splendid, as Henry of Derby discovered. On his journey eastwards, the vanguard fell in with marauding knights in Westphalia and were beaten and robbed, while he himself was seized and held to ransom for 30,000 gold crowns. When he arrived in Prussia, a truce had been declared, and he almost certainly did not have a chance to fight, though a late chronicle embroiders the story of his expedition with a victory in which the Earl himself rescued the Christian standard. On his return journey there were further plots to kidnap him for ransom, and a year later the whole affair ended with a duel at Paris between Henry and Otto of Brunswick, whom he had accused of conspiring against him.

By the fourteenth century, as the story of Henry of Derby's expedition bears out, the Teutonic knights were by no means engaged in continuous warfare, but had become one of the most powerful states in Eastern and Central Europe. Whereas the Hospitallers had only Rhodes as sovereign territory, and relied on the goodwill of other rulers for much of their revenue, the Teutonic knights were lords of a rich countryside, well able to provide for their needs even during expensive campaigns. After the conversion of the Grand Duke of Lithuania in 1386 and his marriage to the Queen of Poland, campaigns no longer had the title of crusades, and the order became more and more a purely territorial power, deeply involved in commercial dealings with the merchants of the Hansa from north Germany (whom they helped by driving the pirates out of Gotland in 1398) and more concerned with the economics of corn production or timber growing than the crusade against the vanishing heathen. On the other hand, the order could not ignore its past and its military tradition. Lithuania had always been its traditional enemy, and Grand Duke Jagiello's conversion and marriage was in fact a political move directed against the order, and designed to check the expansionist ambitions of the knights. A series of broken truces and much skulduggery on both sides followed, and it was clear that the fragile peace could not last for long. Jagiello, now called Wladeslaw II of Poland, harassed the knights by closing their subjects' trading outlets in his new kingdom, and tried to foment unrest inside Prussia. In 1409, a border dispute led to open war, and in 1410 Wladeslaw called on every available enemy of the order: Poles and Lithuanians were accompanied by Cossacks, Tartars, Czechs and Hungarians. Among the commanders of this vast conglomeration were the future Khan of the Golden Horde and Jan Zizka, who was to be the military genius of the Hussites in their religious wars. The Grand Master of the Teutonic knights mobilised all his available reserves and set out to meet the invaders, without waiting for the Livonian knights to join him. He was probably anxious to protect his rich lands from the ravages of the invaders, and was also aware that the Poles were capable of besieging his most powerful castles with some hope of success. On the other hand, his castles were well garrisoned, and the Polish army was so large and loosely organised that it was unlikely to hold together for more than a few months.

The two armies met at Grünwald or Tannenberg at midday on 15 July, in wooded rolling hills. Here the order's cavalry was at a disadvantage; their heavy horse were at their best on the plains, while the Polish horse were lightly armed and therefore better able to manoeuvre in restricted conditions. At first it seemed as if there might be a parley, but the Grand Master ordered his herald to take two swords to Witold, Wladeslaw's deputy in Lithuania, as a symbolic challenge to fight. The knights charged, and drove the Lithuanian left wing off the field; but the centre and right held, while the knights who had pursued the Lithuanians were attacked by Russian and Polish troops. A stalemate ensued, and the Grand Master had to throw in his reserves in a desperate effort to break the Polish line. This failed, and the battle became a hand-to hand mêlée in which superior numbers eventually told. The Grand Master and his senior officers were surrounded and killed, and although the remaining knights tried to rally and retrieve the battle, they were at length forced to flee at the end of a six-hour struggle. The heirs of the heathen had won the day.

Even if the order had won, it could not have benefited from a victory. It had become an anachronism, its purpose was gone; and although it survived for another century and a half, the closing years of its history are a gradual slide into secularism. Although the swift action of one of its officers, Heinrich von Plauen, prevented the Poles from overrunning the order's lands, and the peace of 1411 cost it very little territory, the damage was done: the order could no longer draw on the old sources of recruits who would make 'good monks in the cloister and stern soldiers in the field' now that their campaigns were against fellow Christians. Mercenaries were used to replace the missing recruits; they proved expensive and unreliable, so that taxes were increased and the efficiency of the army declined. Changes in society meant that there was increasing pressure from the towns and from native Prussian nobles (who were debarred from joining the order) for independence of action and a more liberal government. These were encouraged by the Poles to form the Prussian League, and in 1454, the Leaguers allied themselves with the Poles to make war on the order, offering the invented 'Crown of Prussia' to Casimir IV of Poland. The order had always been a strict lord and master, and the Leaguers looked with envy at the freedom, verging on chaos, in which the Polish nobles lived. They were not to achieve it easily, however: the war raged for twelve years, until both League and order were exhausted. In 1466, Casimir was able to annex West Prussia and reduce the Grand Master to a Polish vassal, ruling East Prussia only. The Reformation finished Casimir's work for him: the last Grand Master, Albrecht of Brandenburg, turned the remaining territories into a secular Protestant state in 1525. The Livonian lands, which had become a separate entity after 1466, became a secular duchy in 1591. The order itself survived as a military force until 1697, fighting the Turks in Eastern Europe, notably at the siege of Vienna in 1683.

The history of the military orders may at times seem far removed from the world of chivalry, but in some ways the orders were the nearest that the ideals of chivalry ever came to realisation. Perhaps because of their high aspirations and frequent failures they are still controversial: the Teutonic knights, who were to the nineteenth-century German historian Treitschke 'conquerors, endowed with the triple pride of Christians, Knights and Germans', are anathema to a modern nationalist Polish or Lithuanian historian or to a Marxist scholar. The trial of the Templars still arouses argument, and even the Hospitallers are controversial, despite the fact that they carried out charitable work for longest, and had the highest reputation. It is difficult to depict with equal force the everyday life and work of the orders when the high points of their history are so dramatic: but beside the spectacle of the Teutonic knights clubbing down the heathen, we must set their work in administration and in the colonisation of the order's territory by settlers from Germany, for whom it provided elaborate and far-sighted schemes, designed to ensure their welfare by advanced town planning and yet giving them a considerable degree of freedom. Against the obstinacy and short-sightedness of the Templar Grand Masters in the kingdom of Jerusalem we must set not only the dramatic and courageous defence of Acre, but the building and garrisoning of the great castles that were the bulwark of the kingdom and the raising of endless money and men for the cause of the Christians in, the East. The Hospitallers, even though they turned pirate themselves at times, kept the seas clear of corsairs; and, paradoxically, the finest legacy of the military orders is their charitable work in maintaining the great hospitals which gave them their popular name.

The monastic orders faced repeated crises of a spiritual nature during the Middle Ages, so it is scarcely surprising to find the military orders in the same plight, faced with vastly greater temptations. In both cases, much of the difficulty came from the very enthusiasm with which pious donors gave lands and money to either monks or brethren. However, the monks, particularly the more recluse-like orders, were protected from some of the worldly temptations which faced the orders. Not least of these was the sheer power which the Master of a great order could wield. Instead of a feudal army bound to service by increasingly loose ties and demanding cash payments for any campaign abroad, they commanded élite troops, who had sworn 'obedience unto death'. It is remarkable that the orders did not aim more openly at secular power, and that no Templar or Hospitaller principalities appeared in the East. Their rulers were perhaps wise enough to sense the dangers of secular power; the Teutonic knights in Prussia became a byword not only for their zeal but also for commercial acumen – 'If you're so clever, go and trick the lords of Prussia', said the German proverb. Fierce criticism was also levelled at the high style in which the Teutonic Grand Master lived, and the capital of the order, Marienburg, was one of the most impressive towns of the age, dominated by the castle of the Grand Master which had a beautiful Gothic chapel dedicated to Our Lady, patron of the order. But the Grand Masters were indeed secular princes, and great merchants as well as heads of a religious order, and outward pomp and show was essential in order to impress lesser mortals. The problem was similar in Rhodes, where the hostels of the different nations at times became miniature palaces. Today the castle at Rhodes survives only in a reconstruction ordered by Mussolini, while Hitler restored Marienburg.

One aspect of the orders' place in medieval society has received relatively little attention. For the younger son of a noble family the orders offered an opportunity to make a career as a soldier which neither the feudal armies nor the haphazard life of a mercenary could match. Such men were probably financially unable to marry, and so the vow of celibacy was not necessarily a hardship. The military quality of the orders was never called in question, and this alone signifies that their recruits were of a high standard, though the strict discipline and good training they were given would in itself have been a considerable advantage in an age when an ordinary knight's training was rarely formally organised. Until well into the thirteenth century it was possible for a non-noble to enter the orders, and competition for entry seems to have been keen.

Because the members of the orders rarely wrote about themselves there is one short chronicle by a thirteenth-century Templar, and all the other works by members of the orders are much later – we have to turn to the rule of the orders and their formal documents to gain some picture of life in the orders. Something of the way of life and spirit of the orders emerges from the rule of the Hospitallers, as for example in the address to a candidate who wished to enter the order:

> Good friend, you desire the company of the House and you are right in this, for many gentlemen earnestly request the reception of their children or their friends and are most joyful when they can place them in this order. And if you are willing to be in so excellent and so honourable a company and in so holy an order as that of the Hospital, you are right in this. But if it is because you see us well clothed, riding on great chargers and having everything for our comfort, then you are misled, for when you would desire to eat, it will be necessary for you to fast, and when you would wish to fast, you will have to eat. And when you would desire to sleep, it will be necessary for you to keep watch, and when you would like to stand on watch, you will have to sleep. And you will be sent this side of the sea and beyond, into places which will not please you, and you will have to go there. It will be necessary for you therefore to abandon all your desires to fulfil those of another and to endure other hardships in the order, more than I can describe to you.

Even if the brethren of the order were career soldiers in one sense, they were also very much monks in their daily life. They observed the monastic hours, and even the *auberges* at Rhodes, however lavishly furnished, were arranged on monastic lines. Daily life for a Hospitaller would have been little different from that of the Augustine canons and Cistercian monks, on whose rules the Hospitaller rule was based. Between the numerous daily and special services, which included processions every Sunday and on feastdays, the brethren would attend to their duties as soldiers, just as the Cistercians would attend to their manual labour or the Augustinians to their parochial duties.

Like the monks and canons, members of the orders were vowed to poverty, and their property passed to the order. Because the brethren had business in the outside world rather more frequently than monks, it was easier for them to get round the restrictions of this vow, and we have seen how the luxury of secular chivalry invaded the religious orders. Yet the ideal remained, and a period of laxity was often followed by reform and return to a strict rule: the Hospitallers who in the late thirteenth century 'tried to get their clothes made in a fashionable cut, desired to use a better cloth, sported embroidered kerchiefs and turbans, wore bright colours, especially in silk, had their clothes stitched in gold or silver thread and displayed jewellery', were duly censured by the Chapter General. But when even the admission ceremony describes the brethren as 'well clothed', it is clear that in this area it was usually the knights' secular tastes which overcame their vows; and this is supported by the evidence of Templar retinues, of the Spanish knights in splendid secular costume, and of the Teutonic knights' magnificent receptions for visitors to Prussia.

The military orders are the one truly unique institution produced by European chivalry. Knighthood itself, the idea of an elite warrior caste, can be paralleled in other civilisations; but nowhere else do we find warrior-monks whose fighting capacity is the reason for their taking religious orders. In the East, degenerate monks might become warriors, just as the occasional abbot was to be found at the head of his men on Western battlefields; but only in the military orders did warriors become monks in order to fight a holy war. It is a pity that we do not have the orders' own early chronicles, for much of what we know about them comes from hostile or unsympathetic sources. If we could recover their detailed history, we might well find that the great episodes in the desperate sieges of Acre, Rhodes and Malta were matched by many lesser tales of courage; for at their best the military orders could inspire their knights to a fearless dedication, regardless of self, in the cause of the chivalry of Heaven.

 # From Knight to Gentleman

Subtle yet decisive changes took place in the political and social structure of Western Europe between the twelfth and fifteenth centuries. It was transformed from a loosely unified entity, linked by a common religion and by the institutions of the Church, into an often sharply divided group of nation-states, whose secular organisation had become much more complex: there is a vast difference between an eleventh-century king of France and an early Renaissance ruler like Louis XI. The effect of these changes on chivalry was to transform it from an individual, literary, and slightly unreal ideal into an institution which was part of the new secular state itself, instead of the idea of a universal 'order' of knighthood which the Church had put forward, each state had its own specific order of outstanding knights, obedient to king or prince.

The idea of a secular order of knighthood is first found in literary sources; just as the other ideals of chivalry were first proposed by poets, so the first model for a secular order appears in the romances of Arthur. The Round Table, however, like so many features in the romances, was never a precise institution with elaborate statutes. The main versions of the story of Arthur agree that it came to him as part of Guinevere's dowry: it could seat one hundred and fifty knights, and when Arthur received it, it already had a hundred knights as its fellowship, and these were given to Arthur with the table. A further forty-eight knights were then added, leaving two vacant seats which were the cause of later adventures. One of the seats, the Siege Perilous, was under an enchantment: any knight who sat in it was struck dead, unless he was the chosen knight without peer for whom it was predestined. Otherwise the only qualification for ordinary membership was that a knight had been chosen by Arthur to fill a place made vacant by the death of another. The granting of such a privilege bound a knight to serve Arthur faithfully, but this was an unwritten obligation.

In the thirteenth and fourteenth centuries, occasionally tournaments called 'tables rondes' were held. These seem to have involved the swearing of a kind of oath of brotherhood for the duration of the proceedings, but nothing more. However, in the mid-fourteenth century, Edward III, who was an enthusiastic jouster, gave a new meaning to the idea of a Round Table. He had spent most of 1343 taking part in tournaments: he was thirty and at the height of his skill. During this year the idea of a more permanent society for holding tournaments evidently came to mind, to replace the haphazard arrangements usually made. So at the end of the year he summoned knights and ladies from far and wide, and the chief citizens of London and their wives, to assemble at Windsor for a great feast on 19 January 1344. Elaborate preparations had been made, and rich robes had been provided, including special tunics for the king, his minstrels and two hundred of his squires and men-at-arms. The proceedings opened with a great banquet in the castle hall for the ladies, who included the queen, the queen mother and nine countesses: Prince Edward, the barons and knights ate in tents. In the evening there was dancing and three days of jousting followed in which the king himself was generally acclaimed as the champion, 'not out of flattery but because of his hard work and good luck'.

When the jousts were over, the king made an announcement. No one was to leave that evening, but all were to gather again the next day. Early the following morning, the king, splendidly dressed and wearing his crown, with the queen at his side in magnificent robes and likewise crowned, went to hear Mass. After the service he went in procession with all his nobles to the place arranged for the gathering. Here he swore on the gospels that he would found a Round Table 'of the same kind and status as that laid down by Lord Arthur once king of England, that is to the number of three hundred knights…'. His lords swore a similar oath; then drums and trumpets sounded and everyone went off to another great feast. The date for the gathering of the Round Table was fixed at Whitsun, the usual date for the holding of the original Round Table in the romances; and preparations went forward for the building of a special hall to house it, to be built regardless of cost. In the autumn of 1344, as much as £100 a week was being spent; but the gathering clouds of renewed war with France put an end to such peacetime extravagances, and the proposed Order of the Round Table never came into existence.

Secular associations of knights were by no means unknown: the *hermangildas* in Spain were bands of local gentry who sometimes took religious vows and undertook to protect Christians, and a similar idea lay behind a scheme put forward by John, duke of Normandy, later king of France, which Pope Clement VI approved on 5 June 1344. By six bulls of that date he approved the building of a collegiate church which was to have twenty-four canons and a fellowship of two hundred knights attached to it. The knights were to take the Virgin and St George as their patron saints, and were to meet on their feastdays, 'not for jousting or tournaments or any other deeds of arms,' but for worship. This is clearly a religious confraternity rather than an 'order' with specific rules, but like the Round Table, the renewal of war prevented the scheme from being carried out.

The first purely secular orders of knighthood proper appear to have been formed in Hungary in 1326 and in Spain in 1330. The information is scant and not always reliable; we have little more than the statutes of the Hungarian order of St George, and there are a number of problems attached to the one source which describes the foundation of the Spanish Order of the Sash, the official chronicle of Alfonso XI of Castile. This is largely a contemporary account, but seems to have been revised in 1360–70, that is, after other orders had been founded. The date, therefore, may have been altered to establish the priority of the Castilian order, and as there are virtually no Castilian official documents surviving from the period, there is no reliable confirmation of the story. A list of the early knights does survive, but again it is difficult to check these against the rare surviving official sources, though one or two do appear in the English records in the 1340s and 1350s. On the whole, however, the absence of any positive evidence to the contrary means that we must accept the date of 1330 as genuine, thus making the Order of the Sash the first known secular order.

Its creation arose out of the specific circumstances of Castilian politics at the time. Alfonso XI was deeply engaged in the Reconquista of Spain but he was also embroiled in complex political problems within his kingdom, many of them to do with his personal favourites, in particular his mistress Leonor de Guzman. He needed a corps of knights tied to him by strong personal bonds of loyalty, who would act as the crack regiment of his army and would be loyal and peaceable at court. The orders of Santiago and Calatrava were too powerful and independent (and their knights were rarely at court) for them to fill this role, so Alfonso instituted his own order, as the chronicler tells us:

The king being at Vittoria, because in times past the men of his kingdoms of Castile and León had always practised chivalry, and he had been told that they did not do so in his day, in order that they might be more eager to practise it, he commanded that some knights and squires of his household should wear a sash on their surcoats, and he, the king, would do likewise. And being at Vittoria he sent orders to those knights and squires whom he had chosen for the purpose to wear surcoats with, on them, the sash which he had given them. And he also put on a surcoat with a sash: the first surcoats made for the purpose were white, and the sash vermilion. And from then on he gave each of these knights two surcoats with sashes each year. And the sash was as broad as a man's hand, and was worn over cloaks and other garments from the left shoulder to the waist [that is diagonally]: and they were called the Knights of the Sash [*de la Banda*] and had statutes among themselves on many good matters, all of which were knightly deeds. And when a knight was given the sash, he was made to swear and promise to keep all the things that were written in that book of statutes. And the king did this so that men, wishing to have that sash would have reason to do knightly deeds. And it happened afterwards that if a knight or squire did some feat of arms against the king's enemies, or tried to perform such a feat, the king gave him a sash and did him high honour, so that all the others wished to do good knightly deeds to gain that honour and the goodwill of the king, like those who already had it.

The rules of the order also survive, though only in late copies. These show that the prime object of the order was to provide a nucleus for the royal army: one rule provides for the Knights of the Sash forming one squadron in the royal army on campaign, while others stipulate that knights must have proper equipment and must avoid gambling while on campaign. Tournaments were also an important part of their activities, and the rules end with regulations for the organisation of tournaments and jousts. Alfonso XI himself was reputedly very expert in the lists. The knights are bound together not only by membership of the order and by their common interest in matters of arms, but by an elaborate and solemn oath of loyalty to the king and to each other.

Another order which has a claim to be one of the first secular orders is that of St Catherine, from the Dauphiné in south-east France, probably founded in the 1330s. Knights of this order, who were to carry a shield depicting their patron saint, took a general oath to obey the statutes of the order. These provided that the knights should always have the best interests of the Lord of Dauphiné at heart, and should help each other in all possible ways. They were always to be ready to serve their lord, and tournaments evidently played some part in the order's existence, as knights were to lend each other armour and horses on such occasions. All able-bodied knights within three days' journey of the Chapel of St Catherine at Côte St André were to be there on the vigil and feast of St Catherine. The order was designed to foster 'good love, good faith and good affection between the lord and his knights'.

Neither the Order of the Sash nor the Order of St Catherine had a particularly successful existence; indeed, all we have for the latter is a very late copy of its statutes. The Order of the Sash appears at intervals in the chronicles of Castile during the reigns of Alfonso XI and Pedro the Cruel. At Nájera most of the knights seem to have fought for Pedro's enemy, Enrique of Trastamare, and their standard-bearer, Pero Lopez de Ayala, was not only captured there, but later wrote an account of the battle. The Knights of the Sash fought on foot in the vanguard, and the standard of the order was the rallying-point for Enrique's troops until they were finally routed; many of the knights were killed or captured. The order survived into the fifteenth century, and its insignia appeared on the gold coins of Castile; but it seems to have fallen into disuse, as an unsuccessful attempt was made to revive it in the early sixteenth century.

The first order about which we have certain information on its foundation is that of the Garter, the most famous and certainly the most enduring of all secular orders of knighthood. Even here the exact year of foundation is not certain. The most likely date is 23 April 1348, though the earliest account of the ceremony and the first statutes give 1350 and 1349 respectively. Geoffrey le Baker, a contemporary chronicler, describes the occasion for us:

This year, on St George's Day, the king held a great feast at Windsor Castle, where he instituted a chantry with twelve priests and founded an almshouse in which impoverished knights, for whom their own means did not suffice, might have adequate sustenance in the service of the Lord from the perpetual alms of the founders. Others beside the king were fellow-sureties for the foundation of this almshouse, namely the king's eldest son, the Earl of Northampton, the Earl of Warwick, the Earl of Suffolk, the Earl of Salisbury and other barons; and ordinary knights namely Roger Mortimer, now Earl of March, Sir Walter Mauny, Sir William FitzWarin, John Mohun, John Beauchamp, Walter Paveley, Thomas Wale and Hugh Wrottesley, whose tried worth associated them with the most noble earls. They were all clothed like the king in cloaks of russet powdered with garters, dark blue in colour, and also had similar garters on their right legs, with blue mantles bearing shields of the arms of St George. Dressed like this, they heard Mass bare-headed, celebrated by the Bishops of Canterbury, Winchester and Exeter, and similarly they sat at table together in honour of the holy martyr, from whom they especially took the title of this most noble brotherhood, calling the company of these men of 'St George de la gartiere'.

Baker rightly emphasises the religious aspect of the newly-founded order. The statutes, which were probably prepared during the following year, are hardly concerned with secular affairs at all, the only such clauses being that the Knights of the Garter shall not leave England without permission, that they shall never fight on opposite sides, and that no member of the order is to appear in public without his insignia. The central function of the order is the maintenance of the college of canons and poor knights at Windsor. No knight was to pass through Windsor without hearing Mass at the chapel of the order, and all the knights were to gather for the annual feast of St George's day; if the king gave them leave of absence they were to observe the festival just as carefully as if they had been present.

The number of knights was very small: twenty-five including the king. The Order of the Sash makes no mention of a limit on numbers, and the otherwise similar proposals of John Duke of Normandy of 1344 were for a membership of two hundred knights. As a result the Garter knights formed a very close-knit group around the king. The Black Prince and his companions predominated, and the members were mostly younger than the king. In general, the order was made up of the rising generation of the English commanders in the French wars, men who might well meet in the lists in peacetime or fight side by side in wartime. This underlying link is

Lead badge with the Garter depicting the Black Prince worshipping the Trinity

reflected by a clause in the statutes which says that the king shall 'prefer' Knights of the Garter if any military expedition is in hand; but the military aspect of the order is otherwise not stressed in the foundation documents.

Why was the insignia of the order chosen? A garter was an unusual article of clothing, still regarded as new-fangled at the end of the century; and indeed there is only one mention of the word in English before its appearance in connection with the order. Later legend, perhaps inspired by French propaganda aimed at discrediting the order, told how it was really a homage to one of Edward III's mistresses. Polydore Vergil wrote two hundred years later:

> But the reason for founding the order is utterly uncertain; popular tradition nowadays declares that Edward at some time picked up from the ground a garter from the stocking of his queen or mistress, which had become unloosed by some chance, and had fallen. As some of the knights began to laugh and jeer on seeing this, he is reputed to have said that in a very little while the same garter would be held by them in the highest honour. And not long after, he is said to have founded this order and given it the title by which he showed those knights who had laughed at him how to judge his actions. Such is popular tradition. English writers have been modestly superstitious, perhaps fearing to commit lèse-majesty, if they made known such unworthy things; and they have preferred to remain silent about them, whereas matters should really be seen otherwise: something that rises from a petty or sordid origin increases all the more in dignity.

The story may have a grain of truth in it, but there were also practical and political grounds for both garter and motto. The garter, like the sash, is easily worn *over* armour as a distinguishing mark and allows knights to retain their personal shields, which the Order of St Catherine did not. The inscription and the blue and gold colouring almost certainly refer to Edward's claim to the French throne, blue and gold being the French colours, and the motto, 'Evil to him that evil thinks of it', a reproof to those who challenged his rights.

The Order of the Garter's success was in large measure due to the high standing of its first members, leaders of the English triumphs in France in the 1360s and 1370s. It was also highly exclusive, and therefore became an honour which transcended mere rank: its first members included relatively humble knights, while only three earls were admitted. Another pointer to its future character was the inclusion of three foreign knights who had furthered the

English cause in France: the Order of the Garter and indeed other secular orders were to be important diplomatic weapons.

Other orders now sprang up thick and fast. Some, like the ill-starred Order of the Star in France, involved impractical vows; in this case the knights swore never to retreat in battle. One chronicler says that over half its knights were killed in a single ambush in Brittany in 1353, but in fact it was probably the French defeat at Poitiers in 1356 which undermined the Order of the Star just as it established the reputation of the victorious knights of the Order of the Garter.

The character of the Order of the Garter changed considerably in the early fifteenth century. Henry IV, anxious to secure his title to the English throne, used the Garter as a means of cementing alliances with foreign princes, and awards of this kind became relatively frequent in the fifteenth and sixteenth centuries: some fifty-one foreign sovereign princes were members of the order during this period. When the great Burgundian Order of the Golden Fleece was founded it was closely modelled on the Order of the Garter, having twenty-five knights, though this soon became thirty and later fifty. There were more complex motives behind this foundation, which Philip the Good instituted at his marriage to Isabella of Portugal in 1430, than those of Edward III in founding the Order of the Garter. Philip ruled a disparate collection of lands, divided by different languages, traditions and interests, and he was anxious to create a truly Burgundian nobility, the members of which would owe allegiance to himself rather than to the lands from which they came. In a sense, the purpose of the Golden Fleece was nearer to that of the Order of the Sash, personal loyalty to the ruler being paramount. But Philip needed a council rather than a bodyguard, and the Knights of the Golden Fleece were 'an inner circle of privileged courtiers, councillors and captains', who were able to advise (and even to criticise him) on political matters, though they had no actual political power and met only once a year. The insignia, like that of the Garter, may have had an underlying political meaning, being a compliment to the great weaving towns of the Netherlands, over whom the Duke maintained a sometimes tenuous hold. The order, like the Garter, was also used as a diplomatic weapon (for which the statutes had to be altered so that foreigners could be admitted), and it is interesting to contrast these very practical considerations with the high-flown language of the foundation charter:

To do reverence to God and to uphold the Christian faith, and to honour and increase the noble order of chivalry; and also for the three following reasons: first, to honour older knights whose noble and high deeds are worthy of recognition; second, that those who are now strong and able-bodied; and exercise deeds appropriate to chivalry every day, may have cause to continue them even better than before; and third, that knights and gentlemen who see this order worn ... may be moved to noble deeds themselves and lead such a life that their valiance will earn them great fame, and they will deserve to be chosen to wear the said order: my lord the Duke has undertaken and set up an order called 'La Toison d'Or' [that is, the Golden Fleece].

With the passing of the Burgundian lands to Spain, the order became part of the Spanish court's elaborate system of precedence, and the last general chapter in the Netherlands took place in 1559, although members of the order were still on the governing council for the Spanish Netherlands in the eighteenth century.

Following the success and prestige of the Garter and the Golden Fleece, numerous minor national orders sprang up; every sovereign had to have one or more such orders at his disposal. Their proliferation rapidly led to their debasement; only those severely limited in numbers retained any prestige, and in any case the recipients were no longer knights in anything but name. A general concept of 'titles of honour' had replaced the old chivalric ideal of a universal order of knighthood with a distinct function in society. Furthermore, the corporate spirit of the smaller orders could not exist in orders whose members might run into hundreds or even thousands, and whose fellow-members could only recognise each other by their insignia.

Chivalry had become a servant of the state in other respects. With the increasing emphasis on the sovereign as the 'fount of honour', and the use of formal distinctions between knights who would once have been on equal terms, chivalry became much more closely involved with rank and prestige. Tournaments, partly because they were so expensive, were the prerogative of great rulers and princes by the fifteenth century. They became part of pageants designed to impress by their magnificence both the prince's own subjects and watching envoys from other countries. These great festivals go back to the mid-fourteenth century when the Black Prince, returning from France with King John as his captive, was on his way to London. On the road from Salisbury, five hundred knights disguised as robbers staged a mock ambush, and when the Prince reached London he was met by the city guilds and rode through streets hung with armour, whose fountains ran with wine; and in Cheapside two beautiful girls sat in a kind of birdcage suspended from a goldsmith's shop, scattering gold and silver leaves on the heads of the cavalcade below. It was a scene not unlike that displayed for Charles II at his coronation three hundred years later, and whose distant descendant is the Lord Mayor's pageant of today. Such spectacles, in their most developed form, might involve architecture, painting, sculpture, literature and drama.

These spectacles centred on and spotlighted the figure of the Prince himself. As the struggle for power between Prince and nobles was gradually resolved in the Prince's favour, so chivalry, the nobles' ideal way of life, was used as a way of keeping them entertained and drawing them away from the real world of politics. This was achieved partly by making tournaments elaborate and expensive affairs which nobles could not hope to hold on their own initiative; the emphasis once again passed from the lesser lords who had organised tournaments in the thirteenth and even the fourteenth centuries to the prince as the central figure of chivalry. The transition was made easier by the tradition of making tournaments occasions for disguise and by providing elaborate 'stories' based on the romances. But neither the romances, as exemplified by Philip II's Flemish tournament of 1549, nor the pastoral tradition, as in René d'Anjou's *Pas d'armes de la bèrgiere* of 1449, were really in tune with the new intellectual mood; and instead of Arthurian knights we find references to the Roman *equites*, to harmonise with the rest of the pageant, which was often modelled on the triumphs granted by the Roman senate to a general returning from a successful campaign. Writers on chivalry sought to trace the development of knighthood from classical times, and elaborate 'classical" jousting armour was made, modelled on Roman armour and engraved with scenes from classical mythology. The fighting itself became more and more a formality for, as Henry Peacham wrote in 1634: 'Running at the tilt is a generous and a Martiall exercise, but hazardous and full of danger, for so many hereby (even in sport) have lost their lives, that I may omit *Henry* the French king, with many other princes and other noble personages of whom History is full.' Henri II of France had been killed when the Constable de Montgomeri, against whom he was jousting, failed to drop the broken end of a spear and a splinter penetrated his visor. As a result, the tournament had become more and more like fencing; fighting at the barriers, performed on foot with pike or sword, was popular from the fifteenth century onwards, and it was this kind of display that was put on for the queen and the Duc de Montmorency by Elizabeth's courtiers:

> The place with this royall presence replenished, sodeinlie entered the Earle of *Essex*, and with him twelve Gentlemen armed at al peeces and wel mounted. The Earle and his horse was furnished with white cloathe of silver, and the rest in white satin, who (after reverence done to her Majestie) marched to the East side of the Court, & there in troope stood firme. Forthwith entered the Earle of *Rutland* with a like number in like sort armed and apparelled all in blewe, and having presented his reverence staied on the West end. Before either of these Bands one Chariot was drawne, and therein a faire Damsell conducted by an armed Knight, who presented certeine speeches in the French tung unto her Majestie. These Ceremonies past, the Queen commanded the armed men to fall unto fight, which was performed with great courage & commendation, chiefly in the Earle of *Essex*, a noble personage, valorous in Armes, and all other waies of great vertue. Trulie, this action was mervailouslie magnificent, & appeared a sight exceeding glorious to those that wer below looking upward to the Tarrace, wher her Majestie, the Lords and Ladies stood, so pompously apparailed, jewelled and furnished as hardly can bee seen the like in anie Christian Court; as my selfe and other the Actors (at occasions staying from fight) with great admiration did behold and thinke.

Yet the tournament still had a vitality of its own; both the gentlemen who had become expert in this highly skilled sport, and the spectators, from highest courtier to London guttersnipe, contributing to 'the too forward unruliness of many disordered people,' were enthusiastic supporters of it, and the annual Accession Day tilts from 1579 onwards replaced most successfully the vanished popular ceremonies of the Roman Catholics. Both jousters and spectators came in magnificent costume; even the armour was spectacular, as a surviving drawing of that belonging to Sir Henry Lee shows. Sir Henry Lee was the prime mover behind the Accession Day tilts, and they petered out after his retirement in the 1590s. There was a brief chivalric revival in the early part of James I's reign, since his eldest son, Prince Henry, was an enthusiastic jouster, but after his death in 1612 the surviving chivalric tradition re-emerges only in the court masques. Curiously, in France and Italy, the seventeenth century saw a revival of mock warfare on horseback, with feigned fighting by massed troops of horsemen, which brings us full circle to the games in the ninth century under the late Carolingian kings from which the tournament may have developed.

Chivalry had been used by Elizabeth and her courtiers as a replacement for Church spectacles: in the vast Hapsburg empire of Charles V the Burgundian idea of chivalry as a unifying bond between different nations was revived, and chivalric obedience to the Emperor was the theme of numerous spectacles. But as the sixteenth century wore on, European spectacles moved more towards classical and allegorical themes, and the knights played only a minor part. The astonishing development of spectacular scenery replaced the imaginary wonders of romance with real marvels of illusion.

But the imaginary wonders of medieval romance were by no means dispelled by the clear light of Renaissance culture. On the contrary, they flourished anew; whereas in the fourteenth and fifteenth centuries even the

Sketch by Jacopo Bellini for a tournament costume

humblest manuscript was beyond the means of all but the richest merchants and their families, the printing press now brought romances great and small within the reach of a vast new audience. The old masterpieces made the transition from manuscript to book quickly enough: most of the French Arthurian romances appeared in print between 1490 and 1510, while Malory's new version of those stories came off the press within fifteen years of its composition.

The greatest development in the spread of romances was in countries which, until the late fifteenth century, had not been noted for their interest in matters of chivalry, namely, Spain and Italy. The Spanish books were very much in the medieval tradition, partly because this type of work had never been popular in Spain and was therefore a novelty. The most important to appear was *Amadis de Gaula*, originally written in Portugal in the late thirteenth century, and which imitated Arthurian romance' fairly closely, borrowing certain episodes wholesale, including the central plot of Lancelot and Guinevere. *Amadis* itself is a perfectly competent romance in its original version, but demand for more 'adventures of Amadis' led to a series of increasingly improbable sequels. The same happened with lesser romances such as *Palmerin of England*. The spread of this literature had some strange results; the demand for it was such that barely literate people read it avidly – and believed every word, like the priest who, seeing the official licence to print on the title-pages of the romances, regarded them as gospel truth. Other stories are probably apocryphal, but shrewdly satirise the sudden vogue for chivalry. One Simon de Silveira is said to have sworn on the Gospels that every word in *Amadis* was true, and in another household the master of the house found his assembled family weeping; fearing a disaster, he asked what had happened, and one of them pointed to the book they had been reading and answered: 'Sir, Amadis is dead.' Nor were the Spanish alone in their enthusiasm: in France the different books of *Amadis* were printed one hundred and seventeen times between 1540 and 1577, and Italy and Germany also took up the fashion.

Italy also produced its own reworkings of chivalric romance. Until the fifteenth century Italian chivalric literature had been little more than pale imitations of French romance. In the mid-fifteenth century at Ferrara, whose Duke, Hercules I, was a noted jouster, the court poet Matteo Boiardo wrote a new version of the story of Roland, *L'Orlando Innamorato* (*Roland in Love*) which drew on the stock episodes of romance in order to produce an entertaining extravaganza of action. Boiardo is more interested in strangeness than subtlety, but the success of his unfinished poem led his fellow-countryman Ludovico Ariosto to complete it. Ariosto's immense success with *L'Orlando Furioso* (*Roland's Madness*) was due to his skilful blending of excellent poetry with amazing adventures in which his heroes slay their enemies by the thousand, and a nice touch of realism at the emotional climaxes of the poem. The substance, however, is slight enough: Ariosto's poetic skill redeems a plot which has no great merit of its own.

Yet the ideals of chivalry could still attract wholly serious writers; Milton in the seventeenth century was to consider an Arthurian epic, only to reject it in the end as unworthy of his high intentions, but Torquato Tasso in the 1550s found a chivalric theme to his liking in the story of the First Crusade. His *Gerusalemme Liberata (Jerusalem Delivered)* evokes the greatest epic poet of Italy, Virgil, in its opening, just as Ariosto had done; but instead of Ariosto's 'ladies and knights', Tasso invokes

> *The sacred armies and the godly knight*
> *That the great sepulchre of Christ did free.*

His epic is a sacred epic, the only great example of a poem on the religious aspect of chivalry. Tasso had studied the history of the First Crusade, and makes much of historical episodes; yet into this tale of high endeavour he introduces two love stories, of Rinaldo and Armida, and Tancredi and Clorinda. His purpose, however, is not to entertain his audience with tales of courtly love, but to emphasise his Christian theme. Armida and Clorinda are both pagans; Armida is a sorceress, Clorinda a wild Amazon. The passages of love between Rinaldo and Armida are overlaid by magic, and Rinaldo loses prowess by his entanglement instead of gaining in chivalry as a courtly lover would have done. Clorinda never declares any feeling for Tancredi, and is indeed slain by him in battle; all he can do is to baptize her before she dies. Tasso's own attitude to his material seems to have been ambiguous: he was not personally involved or interested in chivalry except in so far as it was a court tradition at Ferrara, going back almost a century to Boiardo's days as court poet. His own background was a mixture of classical Renaissance learning – hence the imitation of Virgil – and of counter-reformation Catholicism, which produced the choice of a serious Christian theme. But his own character, which emerges strongly in the poem, inclined him to a romantic and imaginative style; and chivalry was the motif of the poem which gave him most scope for flights of fancy.

The *Gerusalemme Liberata* is a paradoxical work in other ways: it is written to glorify the Dukes of Ferrara in the style of the best Renaissance panegyrics, yet Tasso also exhorts his patron, in best medieval tradition, to launch a new crusade. The religious element is powerfully presented: Peter the Hermit becomes a kind of spiritual mastermind behind the crusade, a devout priest and prophet who lends support to the crusaders and guides them in critical moments, while Godfrey of Bouillon is the archetypal Christian knight and a great commander. Yet the figures who were to be remembered in later centuries were Tancredi and Rinaldo, the secular heroes of the poem, and the episodes which were most often quoted were the miraculous events devised by Tasso. These acquire a new force in Tasso. Whereas in the earlier chivalric romances the miraculous wonders were rarely explained and often became an end in themselves, Tasso indulges his love of amazing his audience, but works such events into the greater scheme by depicting them as the work of devils – the devils who support the Egyptians who hold Jerusalem and are the counterpart of the hosts of heaven fighting on the crusaders' side. This supernatural element is integrated into the story in the classical style of Virgil or Homer, where the intervention of the gods is taken as a normal part of epic poetry.

All in all, chivalry in Tasso becomes part of a much wider scheme of things, a rather artificial survival in the rich intellectual world of the Renaissance. Armida's love for Rinaldo leads us far beyond the world of courtly love into philosophical and religious questions: Tasso sees this love as the redeeming feature in her otherwise evil and sensual nature, and by it she eventually comes to repentance and conversion, a total reversal of all the attitudes of courtly love.

Edmund Spenser, in *The Faerie Queene*, acknowledges Tasso as his master. The heroic chivalry of the court of Ferrara is replaced by the richly allegorical knighthood of Elizabeth's courtiers, and by a Protestant ethic which assorts ill with some aspects of his material: his description of the 'bower of bliss' is as tempting as anything in Tasso and harks back to the Tristan legends, but he sees physical love as beyond spiritual redemption, and Sir Guyon destroys it and binds the enchantress Acrasie in order to break its spell. Spenser has an even stronger ethical purpose in writing his epic than Tasso: in the letter to Sir Walter Raleigh 'expounding his whole intention' he writes:

> The generall end therefore of this book is to fashion a gentleman or
> noble person in vertuous and gentle discipline: Which for that I conceived

should be most plausible and pleasing, being coloured with an historicall fiction, the which the most part of men delight to read, rather for variety of matter, then for profite of the ensample: I chose the historye of King Arthure, as most fitte for the excellency of his person ... I labour to pourtraict in Arthure, before he was King, the image of a brave knight, perfected in the twelve private morall vertues, as Aristotle hath devised, the which is the purpose of these first twelve bookes: which if I finde to be well accepted, I may be perhaps encouraged to frame the other part of polliticke vertues in his person, after that hee came to be King.

Fortunately for us, Spenser did not adhere too strictly to his plan of a moral allegory, but began to vary it by the use of examples, and the sheer richness of his poetry quickly outran any possibility of a narrow confinement to his original scheme. The sixth book, on courtesy, takes as its plot a series of adventures freely borrowed from Arthurian romance; the attempts to 'fashion a gentleman in vertuous discipline' give way to the telling of exciting stories. On the other hand, Spenser can equally well make his moral point by a direct approach, as in the stanzas on honour in Book II:

> *Who so in pompe of proud estate (quoth she)*
> *Does swim, and bathes himselfe in courtly blis,*
> *Does waste his dayes in darke obscuritee,*
> *And in oblivion ever buried is:*
> *Where ease abounds, yt's eath to doe amis;*
> *But who his limbs with labours, and his mind*
> *Behaves with cares, cannot so easie mis.*
> *Abroad in armes, at home in studious kind*
> *Who seekes with painfull toile, shall honor soonest find.*
> *In woods, in waves, in warres she wonts to dwell,*
> *And will be found with perill and with paine;*
> *Ne can the man, that mould in idel cell,*
> *Unto her happie mansion attaine:*
> *Before her gate high God did Sweat ordaine,*
> *And wakefull watches ever to abide:*
> *But easie is the way, and passage plaine*
> *To pleasures pallace; it may soone be spide,*
> *And day and night her dores to all stand open wide.*

It is for passages such as this, and for the richness of his poetic fancy and language, that Spenser is remembered, rather than for his portrayal of characters and events. Chivalry is only one part of his allegorical schemes, and these schemes are themselves the lesser part of the poem's merits. In the end the outward show is more impressive than the inner meaning, which all too often reminds us of the elaborate mottoes of knights in Elizabethan jousts, so obscure that the spectators were provided with printed explanations of them. Spenser's attempt to revive the epic of chivalry as a vehicle for moral instruction was doomed to failure.

Where high intentions failed, comedy could succeed. Cervantes' *Don Quixote*, separated by a decade or so from *The Faerie Queene*, is the most famous of all burlesques of chivalry, but it is a deeply affectionate burlesque. Cervantes seems to be saying, 'Here is one of the great ideals of humanity, and look what has become of it!' rather than to be attacking the ideal itself. His quarrel is not with chivalry itself, but with the excesses of its devotees. Byron's shaft, that he 'smiled Spain's chivalry away', is neither true nor accurate: Cervantes pricked the bubble of pretentiousness and exaggeration which surrounded chivalry, but he would have regarded chivalry itself as a valid if old-fashioned ideal. His target was 'the authority and welcome which books of chivalry enjoy with the common people', those fantastic overblown romances that poured off the presses in a flood of blackletter pages. Indeed, when the priest goes through Don Quixote's books in order to burn those which have inspired the knight's first fit of chivalric madness, he does not condemn them all to the flames; the barber describes the first book they find, *Amadis de Gaula*, as 'the best of all the books of this kind ever written' and it is reprieved. The romances about Roland and his companions are banished to the bottom of a dry well, while *Palmerin of England* and *Tirant lo Blanch* escape completely, one to be 'kept and treasured as a rarity' because of its excellence, the other because 'for its style it is the best book in the world. Here the knights eat and sleep and die in their beds, and make their wills before they die, and other things as well that are left out of all other books of the kind.' As for those which are burnt, the Canon of Toledo describes their extravagances in his tirade against them:

What beauty can there be, or what harmony between the parts and the whole, or between the whole and its parts, in a book or story in which a sixteen-year-old lad deals a giant as tall as a steeple one blow with his sword, and cuts him in two as if he were made of marzipan? And when they want to describe a battle, first they tell us that there are a million fighting men on the enemy's side. But if the hero of the book is against them, inevitably, whether we like it or not, we have to believe that such and such a knight gained the victory by the valour of his strong arm alone. Then what are we to say of the ease with which a hereditary queen or empress throws herself into the arms of an unknown and wandering knight? What mind not totally barbarous and uncultured can get pleasure from reading that a great tower, full of knights, sails out over the sea like a ship before a favourable wind, and that one night it is in Lombardy and by dawn next morning in the land of Prester John of the Indies, or in some other country that Ptolemy never knew nor Marco Polo visited?

Notice how the standing of the chivalry books has sunk! The men who once wrote and read them avidly, the canons and educated men, are now their bitterest critics, applying the rules of Renaissance taste to these exuberant edifices of fiction. It is the innkeeper who defends them, and part of Don Quixote's madness is that as an intelligent and educated man he takes seriously what everyone else has long since given up as fantasy. Yet in order to portray this madness, Cervantes needed a thorough knowledge of books of chivalry: indeed, he was by no means so averse to them as his criticisms might lead us to believe, and Salvador de Madariaga has suggested that the whole of *Don Quixote* had its origins in a perfectly serious attempt by Cervantes to write an orthodox romance of chivalry.

But once Cervantes has burnt his books of chivalry, there arises out of the ashes a new ideal, an ideal which he does not state directly. Lancelot and Guinevere, Tristan and Iseult, had been the ideals of love in medieval romances; Perceval and Galahad had stood as shining examples of spiritual attainment. Cervantes now rejects the framework in which such ideal figures appeared, and offers us an anti-hero; but in his anti-hero's faults he draws a kind of negative image of the ideals he admires – reason, self-restraint, and moderation. As the defeated knight returns to his village, Sancho sums up their adventures: 'Open your eyes, my beloved country, and see your son Sancho Panza returning – if not rich, yet well beaten. Open your arms and receive your son Don Quixote too, who, though conquered by another, has conquered himself – which, as I have heard him say, is the very best kind of victory.' Self-knowledge and a return to the values of philosophy have taken over from the world of adventures and heroic aspirations.

The change from medieval to Renaissance ideals took time to appear in literature; but it was already well established by Cervantes' day in manuals of behaviour. The old treatises on knighthood had long since been superseded by books which taught new standards, those of the gentleman and courtier. In the fifteenth century, Jacques Le Grand's *Book of Good Manners*, although it carries on the knightly tradition and depicts the perfect knight in orthodox terms, already lays great emphasis on the domestic behaviour of the knight. The first true book of courtesy is Baldassare Castiglione's *The Courtier*, which appeared in 1528, and set the tone for many of the attitudes of the knight's successor, the gentleman. The gentleman's ideals are often assumed to stem from those of chivalry; but in the main this is untrue. The gentleman's models hark back either to the classical world, or to the great men of contemporary life, and many writers on conduct in the sixteenth century are harsh critics of the chivalrous code, condemning duelling and attacking the ethics of the romances. Roger Ascham wrote in the mid-sixteenth century against Malory's works: 'the whole pleasure of which booke standeth in two speciall poyntes, in open mans slaughter, and bold bawdrye: In which booke these be counted the noblest Knightes, that do kill most men without any quarell, and commit foulest adulteries by sutlest shiftes.'

Yet the code of the courtier, which Ascham admired, was little better in ethical terms: for the sins of the flesh – which Ascham's Protestant conscience abhorred- were in some measure replaced by the sins of the spirit. Castiglione's elegant writing conceals the full worldliness of his advice, but the courtier is measured not by his inward devotion to an ideal, but by his appearance of success and his standing in other men's eyes. Reputation is everything, reality counts for little. When reading Castiglione after having read chivalric literature, the absence of a guiding idealism is striking. Here is the courtier in battle, calculating the use of his energy to obtain the best effect:

> If you remember, yesterday evening the Count said he wished the courtier's chief profession to be that of arms, and he spoke at length about the way he should pursue it. So we shall not repeat this. All the same, it should also be understood from the rule I gave that when the courtier finds himself involved in a skirmish or pitched battle, or something of that nature, he should arrange to withdraw discreetly from the main body and accomplish the bold and notable exploits he has to perform in as small a company as possible and in view of all the noblest and most eminent men

of the army, and, above all, in the presence, or if possible under the very eyes, of the prince he is serving. For it is certainly right to exploit the things one does well.

If he happens to engage in arms in some public spectacle, such as jousting, tourneying or volleying, or other kind of physical recreation, mindful of where and in whose presence he is, he will make sure that he is as elegant and attractive in the exercise of arms as he is competent, and that he feeds the eyes of those who are looking on with everything that can give him added grace.

It is a far cry from the French cavalry hurling themselves headlong into battle at Crécy or Nicopolis.

For the knight, his ideals of love or religion – theoretically at least transcended everything else. But a sixteenth-century Lancelot, instead of being reproved by Guinevere for his hesitation in mounting the hangman's cart, was expected to bear in mind his dignity: even harmless amusements like country sports were to be avoided, because 'it would be unbecoming for a gentleman to honour by his personal appearance some country show, where the spectators and participants were common people'. Discretion is the keyword, and the centre of the courtier's world is not his lady but his prince: he should 'devote all his thought and strength to loving and almost adoring the prince he serves above all else, devoting all his ambitions, actions and behaviour to serving him.' Behaviour is indeed the keynote: Castiglione gives careful advice on exactly what kind of conduct is acceptable, the kind of witticisms and jokes that gain favour and those that do not; indeed, the section on wit is one of the longest in the book.

If the prince is the lodestar of the courtier's world, this leaves him little time for women. When one of Castiglione's characters suggests that 'the courtier should above all show respect and reverence for women, especially if there is any question of impugning their honour,' one of his companions retorts: 'Without doubt, Bernardo, you are too partial to women. And why do you want men to show more respect to women than women to men? Isn't our honour perhaps as dear to us as theirs is to them?' Castiglione gives ample room to anti-feminist views which would do credit to a medieval clergyman, but he balances them with a true and careful portrait of the ideal court lady. When it comes to love he is once again insistent on discretion: and there is no trace of idealism in his treatment of the lady's part in it. She must avoid the flatterer who wants only to seduce her, and must be careful not to be too forward in such matters; the ideal lover will be patient and will not parade his love before all, while the lady will respond in kind. Love is an equal partnership, with no trace of exaggerated worship.

The Courtier had a great influence on the shaping of the new ideal of the gentleman, an ideal which was in its way just as literary as that of knighthood in its most elaborate form. Italy was the cultural leader of Europe, its poetry the model for all ambitious writers, whether in France, Spain or England, and *The Courtier* was soon translated into all these languages. 'Gentleman', however, was a looser term than 'knight', and many a citizen who could never have aspired to knighthood became a gentleman by dint of a little discretion about his origins. 'Gentle' birth was different from nobility, for which a title was required; to be a gentleman, you had only to trace your descent from a 'gentle' family for three generations and, as the Spanish put it, you were a *hidalgo*, the son of a person of consequence. The sharpest difference between knight and gentleman, however, was that while a knight was by definition a warrior, the gentleman regarded skill in the use of arms as an accomplishment. Manuals for gentlemen frowned on duels, and the mechanical warrior was a figure of fun. Castiglione has an anecdote to show what the courtier thought of men of mere action:

To these may very fairly be said what a worthy lady once remarked jokingly, in polite company, to a certain man (I don't want just now to mention him by name) whom she had honoured by asking him to dance and who not only refused but would not listen to music or take part in the many other entertainments offered, protesting all the while that such frivolities were not his business. And when at length the lady asked what his business was, he answered with a scowl: 'Fighting.'

'Well then,' the lady retorted, 'I should think that since you aren't at war at the moment and you are not engaged in fighting, it would be a good thing if you were to have yourself well greased and stowed away in a cupboard with all your fighting equipment, so that you avoid getting rustier than you are already.'

Elsewhere, one of his characters warns against excessive enthusiasm for deeds of arms:

Do you not agree that that friend of ours, of whom I spoke to you the other day, had completely forgotten whom he was talking to and why, when, to entertain a lady whom he had never seen before, he began their conversation by announcing that he had slaughtered so many men, how fierce he was, and that he knew how to wield a sword with both hands? And before he left her he was wanting to teach her how certain blows of the battle-axe should be parried, both when one was armed and when one was unarmed, and the various ways of brandishing a sword, until the poor girl was suffering agonies and every moment seemed like an eternity till she could make her escape before being cut down like the others.

The gentleman was a purely social figure, with no specific function; the emphasis had. changed from function and achievement to inherited status, and by the end of the sixteenth century, 'knight' had become a mere title. For a century or more there were

> No Knights o'the Sun, nor Amadis de Gauls
> Primaleons, Pantagruels, public nothings,
> Abortives of the fabulous dark cloister.

Chivalry was to revive once more, but in purely literary form. Heralds, architects, and scholars kept some specialist interest in the Middle Ages alive; Dryden and Pope appreciated Chaucer, and learned writers began to explore the riches of medieval manuscripts. By the mid-eighteenth century, the 'Gothick' was once again esteemed, but it was still far from popular. Furthermore, interest was concentrated on the Norse and Anglo-Saxon works, in particular on the Icelandic sagas. Some translations from these were made in the 1750s, but it was the triumphs of the forged 'Ossian' poems, supposedly the remains of great sagas in the Gaelic tongue, which first attracted public attention to the Middle Ages. James Macpherson, who created 'Ossian', had shrewdly hit on what the public wanted, and with these heroic-romantic poems – which now read as sadly faded and dated verses – the gates of a new world were opened for many readers. Ossian's enthusiasts included figures as diverse as Goethe and Bonaparte, and sounder scholars than Macpherson hastened to supply the new demand for 'ancient' verse. Bishop Percy's *Reliques of Old English Poetry* followed, edited from a manuscript which Percy found being used to light fires. Percy diffidently looked forward to a revival of poetry beyond the ballads which he printed, mostly in late fifteenth-century forms: 'Should the public encourage the revival of some of those ancient Epic Songs of Chivalry, they would frequently see the rich ore of an Ariosto or a Tasso, tho' buried it may be among the rubbish and dross of barbarous times.'

The public did indeed encourage such a revival. Gothic architecture was newly appreciated, and from admiration of the visual arts, men of culture turned to the study of poetry contemporary with the great cathedrals they had come to regard as masterpieces. Thomas Wharton's *History of English Poetry* (1774–81) was the first critical attempt to explore this world, yet both he and Richard Hurd, whose *Letters on Chivalry and Romance* appeared in 1762, were more interested in discussing knight-errantry as an institution or romance as a form – in other words the customs and ideals reflected in medieval literature- than in working on the poems themselves or setting out to map the historical reality. In France, a similar renascence of interest proceeded on more scholarly lines: La Curne de Ste Palaye compiled sixty-one manuscript volumes on medieval French, and in the course of doing so read many of the original romances, which he used for his *Memoires sur l'ancienne chevalerie* (1759–1781), a book which did a great deal to revive interest in the Middle Ages: in particular, he gave abstracts of many of the texts. In England, the collection of actual texts proceeded more slowly: Tyrwhitt's edition of Chaucer (1775) was the first really scientific piece of work to be done, while the irascible and sharp-tongued Joseph Ritson, whose castigations of his fellow-editors still make amusing reading today, edited many of the romances and ballads in the first decade of the nineteenth century.

It was not until after 1800 that this scholarly work began to bear fruit. The Romantic poets were aware of the Middle Ages in a way that their predecessors had never been, and in 1790 even a classical orator like Edmund Burke could evoke the past glories of chivalry in *Reflections on the Revolution in France*:

It is now sixteen or seventeen years since I saw the Queen of France, then the Dauphiness, at Versailles; and surely never lighted on this orb, which she hardly seemed to touch, a more delightful vision. I saw her just above the horizon, decorating and cheering the elevated sphere she just began to move in – glittering like the morning star, full of life, and splendour, and joy . . . Little did I dream that I should have lived to see disasters fallen upon her in a nation of gallant men, in a nation of men of honour, and of cavaliers. I thought ten thousand swords must have leaped from their scabbards to avenge even a look that threatened her with insult. But the age of chivalry is gone. That of sophisters, economists, and calculators, has succeeded; and the glory of Europe is extinguished for ever.

Chivalry, as it emerged in the nineteenth-century revival, had a new meaning, and Burke uses it in this sense: of all the knight's ideals and duties, it is the devotion to women that survives. At first 'chivalry' was revived as a general term for the general attitudes and culture of medieval knights, but these attitudes were quickly idealised into 'a punctilious regard for honour, a generous reverence for justice, and a hatred of injustice.' 'Chivalrous', a word rarely found in the Middle Ages, came to mean someone who embodied these supposedly knightly virtues. Freeman, in his great work on the Norman conquest in 1876, exaggerates this ideal in order to attack it:

> The chivalrous spirit is, above all things, a class spirit. The good knight is bound to endless fantastic courtesies towards men, and still more towards women of a certain rank; he may treat any below that rank with any degree of scorn and cruelty.

He went on to characterise 'the whole chivalrous idea' as quite un-English. But in popular usage, in the novels of Ouida, it was the gallant meaning that won the day, the idea of a disinterested devotion to and idealisation of women, until it became a synonym for courtesy of a slightly exaggerated kind. Kenelm Digby summed it up in his *Broad Stone of Honour*: 'Chivalry is only a name for that general spirit or state of mind which disposes men to heroic and generous actions.'

If medieval writers used either 'chivalry' or 'chivalrous', they had in mind bravery and deeds of arms. What Victorian writers had in mind as chivalry would in the Middle Ages have been called courtesy, but the latter had acquired its own new overtones and implications. The view of chivalry as a kind of nobility of spirit was, of course, much coloured by the novels of Sir Walter Scott and his imitators. As a young man Scott had read the romances, as well as Ariosto and Boiardo in the original and Spenser's *Faerie Queene*: he later said of himself that he 'fastened like a tiger upon every collection of old songs and romances'. His first major publication was followed by an edition of the English Tristan romance, *Sir Tristram*. His first great successes – *The Lay of the Last Minstrel, Marmion* – were poetic, something which is easily forgotten in view of his later overwhelming triumph as a novelist. The romantic and poetic is never far away in his novels, and contributes to the highly coloured picture of chivalry which he paints there: yet it is a consistent and well-informed picture. 'Show me an old castle or a field of battle and I was at home at once, filled it with its combatants in their proper costume and over-whelmed my hearers with the enthusiasm of my description,' he wrote. *Ivanhoe*, whatever its faults in general historical terms, is full of such vivid details; its effect on the popular view of the Middle Ages can be traced down to Hollywood's spectacular attempts to recapture the imagined splendours of a romantic past.

Scott's views on chivalry were summed up in an essay he wrote for the 1818 edition of *Encyclopaedia Britannica*. Defining chivalry at the beginning of his essay, he writes:

In every age and country valour is held in esteem, and the more rude the period and the place, the greater respect is paid to boldness of enterprise and success in battle. But it was peculiar to the institution of Chivalry, to blend military valour with the strongest passions which actuate the human mind, the feelings of devotion and those of love. The Greeks and Romans fought for liberty or for conquest, and the knights of the Middle Ages for God and for their ladies. Loyalty to their sovereigns was a duty also incumbent upon these warriors; but although a powerful motive, and by which they often appear to have been strongly. actuated, it entered less warmly into the composition of the chivalrous principle than the two preceding causes. Of patriotism, considered as a distinct predilec-tion to the interests of one kingdom, we find comparatively few traces in the institutions of knighthood. But the love of personal freedom, and the obligation to maintain and defend it in the persons of others as in their own, was a duty particularly incumbent on those who attained the honour of Chivalry. Generosity, gallantry, and an unblemished reputation, were no less necessary ingredients in the character of a perfect knight. He was not called upon simply to practise these virtues when opportunity offered, but to be sedulous and unwearied in searching for the means of exercising them, and to push them without hesitation to the brink of extravagance, or even beyond it. Founded on principles so pure, the order of Chivalry could not, in the abstract at least, but occasion a pleasing though a romantic development of the energies of human nature.

He deals briefly with the knight and religion, which as a staunch Protestant he labels 'superstition', and moves on to enthuse about the knight and his lady:

> Amid the various duties of knighthood, that of protecting the female sex, respecting their persons, and redressing their wrongs, becoming the champion of their cause, and the chastiser of those by whom they were injured, was represented as one of the principal objects of the institution. Their oath bound the new-made knights to defend the cause of all women without exception; and the most pressing way of conjuring them to grant a boon was to implore it in the name of God and the ladies... The looks, the words, the sign of a lady, were accounted to make knights at time of need perform double their usual deeds of strength and valour. At tournaments and in combat, the voices of the ladies were heard like those of the German females in former battles, calling on the knights to remember their fame, and exert themselves to the uttermost. 'Think, gentle knights,' was their cry, 'upon the wool of your breasts, the nerve of your arms, the love you cherish in your hearts, and do valiantly, for ladies behold you.' The corresponding shouts of the combatants were, 'Love of ladies! Death of warriors! On, valiant knights, for you fight under fair eyes.'

Like most writers on chivalry in the nineteenth century, Scott draws primarily on literary sources for his illustrations; and since these are, by and large, idealisations of real life, he arrives at a distinctly artifical picture of the Middle Ages. The one historian he uses is Froissart, who also idealised his stories and put a comfortable romantic gloss on reality.

Scott's approving view of chivalry was rounded off by a diatribe in which he showed how its decline had brought all kinds of horrors in its wake. But other voices had their doubts about chivalry itself. Byron, in the preface to *Childe Harold*, commented, giving chapter and verse:

> It so happens that the good old times, when '*l'amour du bon vieux tems, l'amour antique*' flourished, were the most profligate of all possible centuries. Those who have any doubts on this subject may consult Sainte-Palaye, *passim*, and more particularly vol. ii p. 69. The vows of chivalry were no better kept than any other vows whatsoever; and the songs of the Troubadours were not more decent, and certainly much less refined, than those of Ovid. The '*Cours d'amour, parlemens d'amour, ou de courtesie et de*

gentilesse,' had much more of love than of courtesy or gentleness. See Roland on the same subject with Sainte-Palaye. Whatever other objection may be urged to that most unamiable personage Childe Harold, he was so far perfectly knightly in his attributes: 'no waiter, but a knight-templar'. By the by, I fear that Sir Tristram and Sir Lancelot were no better than they should be, although very poetical personages and true knights '*sans peur*', though not '*sans reproche*'. If the story of the institution of the 'Garter' be not a fable, the knights of that order have for several centuries borne the badge of a Countess of Salisbury of indifferent memory. So much for chivalry. Burke need not have regretted that its days are over, though Marie Antoinette was quite as chaste as most of those in whose honours lances were shivered and knights unhorsed.

Before the days of Bayard, and down to those of Sir Joseph Banks, (the most chaste and celebrated of ancient and modern times), few exceptions will be found to this statement, and I fear a little investigation will teach us not to regret these monstrous mummeries of the Middle Ages.

Thomas Arnold was even more severe: 'If I were called upon to name what spirit of evil predominantly deserved the name of Antichrist, I should name the spirit of chivalry – the more detestable for the very guise of the 'Archangel ruined' which has made it so seductive to the most generous minds.'

But Arnold's view was a minority one, and the enthusiasm for chivalry aroused by Scott's novels was very real. The most spectacular demonstration of this cult was the episode of the Eglinton tournament of 1839. It arose out of the frugal coronations of William IV and Victoria when, partly for political reasons and partly in reaction against the excesses of George IV's crowning, the state banquet and its traditional ceremonies were abandoned, much to the fury of the backwoodsmen of the House of Lords. But others besides the purely traditionalists were irritated, for the public taste for romance and spectacle was at its height, and the coronation ceremonies promised a genuine event of the best Gothic kind. One of a group of young noblemen interested in medieval matters, the Earl of Eglinton, was rumoured – incorrectly, as it happened – to be planning a medieval tournament; but as the rumour spread Eglinton decided to live up to it. Aided and abetted by his half-brother and step-father, both of whom were medieval enthusiasts to the point of eccentricity, Eglinton announced that he would indeed hold a tournament at Eglinton Castle in the following year, 1839. There had already been rumours of a tournament to mark

*(opposite) Two scenes
from the Eglinton
tournament*

Victoria's accession, and the St James' theatre was presenting a melodrama called *The Tournament*, written by Lord Burghersh. The moment for Eglinton's announcement was perfect. One young blood wrote thirty years afterwards:

> When the Eglinton Tournament was first suggested, I know of nothing that ever seized on the minds of the young men of fashion with such force as it did, or held out apparently so many romantic attractions. I can safely say that, as far as I was concerned, I was seized with an extraordinary desire to be one of those who would enter the lists, without at first considering the consequences which must inevitably attend on such a proceeding. Perhaps, assisted by the narratives of the *Wizard of the North*, and other illustrators of the olden times, all that I thought of for the moment was a Queen of Beauty, brave deeds, splendid arms, and magnificent horses.

Fortunately for Eglinton, some practical work had recently been done on medieval armour, notably by Samuel Meyrick, a leading antiquary who was responsible for the first museum of arms and armour at the Tower of London, opened in 1828, and who had a large private collection. Charles Lamb, Eglinton's half-brother, was another collector, and a shop specialising in armour, designed to revive 'the splendour of our ancient Baronial Halls' opened in Bond Street in 1838. The owner of the shop, Samuel Pratt, was the obvious person to help and advise on the armour necessary for the tournament, and the first meeting to discuss who should take part and how the tournament should be staged was held at Pratt's showroom, a newly-built gallery in the best Gothic style. Eglinton decided that the tournament should be in the fifteenth-century style, consisting of jousting over a tilt, and that the *mêlée*, which was in any case rare in late tournaments, should be replaced by a triumph. Apparently this disappointed some of the would-be participants, because although one hundred and fifty attended the first meeting, only forty or so persevered, and placed provisional orders for their armour.

Equipping a knight for a tournament was an expensive business in the fifteenth century; in Victorian England, where many of the necessary skills had disappeared, the cost was ruinous. Lord Glenlyon spent some £1,500 by the time the tournament was over, instead of the modest £40 or so originally estimated. Nor was money the only problem. Although the competitors were expert horsemen, none of them had ever worn armour or used a lance before. By dint of practice at a specially equipped tilting ground near Regent's Park, they managed to acquire some degree of skill: but what had taken a medieval knight twenty years or so to master could hardly be learnt in a few afternoons tilting at the quintain or at a dummy which ran on a sloping track and was dubbed 'the Railway Knight'. By the time of the dress rehearsal in London at the end of July, however, a reasonable degree of skill had been acquired, even if only nineteen knights had stayed the course. Some knights even broke their spears on their opponents, though these had been carefully cut with a cross grain which made them snap easily. The dress rehearsal was accounted a success and the knights set off for Scotland.

Meanwhile, public interest was at fever pitch, whipped up by continual reports of progress in the newspapers. When the day came, a huge crowd had descended on Eglinton, and every house for miles around had its paying guests, such was the eagerness to see this famous event. There were, however, only thirteen knights for the lists, but everything else appeared to be ready and in good order. The elaborate lists provided open-air seating for four thousand, with a covered grandstand for the 'Queen of Beauty', Lady Seymour, and her attendants in the centre. The ceremonies were to start with a great procession, and it was here that the first problems arose. Not only had a huge crowd, estimated by the journalists at one hundred thousand people, gathered in and around the lists, but no proper plan had been made for the assembly of those taking part. The start of proceedings was announced for noon; it was three o'clock before the knights left the castle. The sky had clouded over as the day wore on, and just as the Queen of Beauty mounted her horse, a peal of thunder marked the beginning of a deluge that lasted for the rest of the day. A medieval tournament would probably have been cancelled on the spot; but since such elaborate arrangements had been made, there was nothing for it but to continue. Much of the ceremonial had to be omitted, and even the covered grandstands were little use against the torrential rain. The lists quickly became a treacherous slippery morass, and as a final disaster the first two knights not only missed each other altogether, but one of them dropped his spear as he attempted to remain in the saddle. Only one of the jousts, between Lord Eglinton himself and Lord Waterford was even moderately successful, Eglinton breaking his spear on his opponent's shield. To add to the disaster, the tent in which the medieval banquet was to be given collapsed, and the banquet had to be cancelled. The unhappy spectators made their way home as best they could.

Two days later, after the damage had been hastily repaired, the jousts were held in proper style and with some success. A kind of medieval mêlée was included, and the banquet and ball were accounted a triumph. All this, however, was not enough to wipe out the memory of the first day's debacle. The Eglinton tournament, which had begun with such extravagant expectations, and which might have been genuinely impressive, ended as a lavish failure, the butt of satirists for decades to come. Even if the weather had been kinder, and the event had succeeded, no one but Lord Eglinton and his ilk could have dreamed of repeating such an occasion. The precise cost is not known; the final bill seems to have been about £40,000. If nothing else, Eglinton had proved that tournaments were not a practical amusement, even for the wealthiest of lords; but a careful reading of fifteenth-century history could have told him that without the expense of actually trying it. Such things were best left to the imagination of Sir Walter Scott:

> *Now caracoll'd the steeds in air,*
> *Now plumes and pennons wanton'd fair,*
> *But soon too earnest grew the game,*
> *The spears drew blood, the swords struck flame,*
> *And, horse and mart, to ground there came*
> *Knights, who shall rise no more!*
> *Gone was the pride that war had graced,*
> *Gay shields were cleft, and crests defaced,*
> *And steel coats riven, and helms unbraced,*
> *And pennons stream'd with gore.*

The public had not done with chivalry, however. When Tennyson, already an established poet, was in search of an epic theme in the 1850s, he returned to the theme which he had first sketched in 1833, and on which he had written about the time of the Eglinton tournament: the legends of King Arthur. When *The Idylls of the King* appeared in 1859 it was an instant success, selling ten thousand copies in the first week. The Arthurian legends were by no means a well-known subject: only one edition of Malory had appeared since the sixteenth century, and some reviewers felt the choice of subject unwise, calling the stories 'a forgotten cycle of fables', and lamenting Tennyson's abandonment of his portrayal of modern life. The majority, however, agreed with Gladstone that Arthur was the greatest of our national and Christian heroes, 'human in the largest and deepest sense', and universal as well as national in the implications of his story. For Tennyson succeeded in touching not only the popular romantic chord of the public's appetite for past glories, but made of Arthur a perfect Victorian gentleman, thus implying that chivalry was a living moral force in imperial Britain. One reviewer said that 'the meadow of Camelot represents the field of the world's battle', and saw in Tennyson's handling of his characters 'the social truths that are of all time'. Tennyson himself felt that he had used the material of the chivalric romances, but had 'infused into the legends a spirit of modern thought and an ethical significance.'

But this very ethical significance led him into difficulties with the topic which earlier romantic writers had taken to be the central point of chivalry – courtly love. Tennyson's hero is Arthur, the peerless king, and Guinevere's love for Lancelot is a betrayal of him both as husband and lord. They become a guilty pair of adulterous lovers, harshly treated by Arthur, and their love is seen as a moral poison which infects the whole court, leading directly to the 'last, dim, weird battle in the west'. Tennyson's prime interest was not in fact in chivalry, though he was fully aware of its possibilities for poetic colour, but in the greater themes which could be woven around Arthur himself. At the end of *The Coming of Arthur* he portrays Arthur and his court in their prime, Christian warriors united against the heathen world, whether Roman or Saxon.

> *There at the banquet those great Lords from Rome,*
> *The slowly fading mistress of the world,*
> *Strode in, and claim'd their tribute as of yore*
> *But Arthur spake,'Behold, for these have sworn*
> *To wage my wars, and worship me their King;*
> *The old order changeth, yielding place to new;*
> *And we that fight for our fair father Christ,*
> *Seeing that ye be grown too weak and old*
> *To drive the heathen from your Roman wall,*
> *No tribute will we pay': so those great lords*
> *Drew back in wrath, and Arthur strove with Rome.*
>
> *And Arthur and his knighthood for a space*
> *Were all one will, and thro' that strength the King*
> *Drew in the petty princedoms under him,*
> *Fought, and in twelve great battles overcame*
> *The heathen hordes, and made a realm and reign'd.*

The tension and drama in the poems lies between the noble natures and intentions of Arthur and his knights and the evil of passionate love which leads to falsehood and treachery. And indeed there is something of truth in Guinevere's description of Arthur as 'high, self-contain'd, and passionless'. In Arthur's farewell to Guinevere, Tennyson describes the king's first hopes and aims, and in so doing sums up not only his own code of chivalry but also the tragedy of Arthur's failure:

> But I was first of all the kings who drew
> The knighthood-errant of this realm and all
> The realms together under me, their Head,
> In that fair Order of my Table Round,
> A glorious company, the flower of men,
> To serve as model for the mighty world,
> And be the fair beginning of a time.
> I made them lay their hands in mine and swear
> To reverence the King, as if he were
> Their conscience, and their conscience as their King,
> To break the heathen and uphold the Christ,
> To ride abroad redressing human wrongs,
> To speak no slander, no, nor listen to it,
> To honour his own word as if his God's,
> To lead sweet lives in purest chastity,
> To love one maiden only, cleave to her,
> And worship her by years of noble deeds,
> Until they won her; for indeed I knew
> Of no more subtle master under heaven
> Than is the maiden passion for a maid,
> Not only to keep down the base in man,
> But teach high thought, and amiable words
> And courtliness, and the desire of fame,
> And love of truth, and all that makes a man.
> And all this throve before I wedded thee,
> Believing, 'lo mine helpmate, one to feel
> My purpose and rejoicing in my joy.'
> Then came thy shameful sin with Lancelot;
> Then came the sin of Tristram and Isolt;

Then others, following these my mightiest knights,
And drawing foul ensample from fair names,
Sinn'd also, till the loathsome opposite
Of all my heart had destined did obtain,
And all thro' thee! so that this life of mine
I guard as God's high gift from scathe and wrong,
Not greatly care to lose; but rather think
How sad it were for Arthur, should he live,
To sit once more within his lonely hall,
And miss the wonted number of my knights,
And miss to hear high talk of noble deeds
As in the golden days before thy sin.

From Knight
to Gentleman

*James Archer, 'The
Death of Arthur': the
epitome of the Victorian
ideal of chivalry*

Tennyson used the Arthurian legends for his own purposes and reshaped their spirit to his own ends; and the Arthurian stories have lived on precisely because they are a mould into which each new generation can pour its own ideals and aspirations. In this, they are both less and more than the chivalry which first trade them famous. Chivalry belongs to history, to the noble ideas which have inspired poets but which have found only a dim reflection in the mirror of real events. We cannot set the quest of the Grail beside the crusades, the love of Lancelot and Guinevere beside that of Paolo and Francesca da Rimini and call them equal: but the same spirit infuses both, and if the romance outstrips the reality, why then

> *a man's reach should exceed his grasp*
> *or what's a heaven for?*

Yet whatever crimes were committed in its name, among all the secular codes of conduct that men have devised for themselves, few have been a match in their aspirations and achievements for the ideals of medieval knighthood that men called chivalry.

Further Reading

For a full bibliography, see Richard Barber, *The Knight and Chivalry* (second edition, Woodbridge and Rochester, NY, 1995).

For readers who wish to pursue individual topics, the following titles may be useful.

KNIGHTS AND KNIGHTHOOD

Peter Coss, *The Knight in Medieval England 1000–1400* (Far Thrupp and Dover, NH, 1993)
Benjamin Arnold, *German Knighthood 1050–1300* (Oxford 1985)
Marc Bloch, *Feudal Society* (tr. L. A. Maryon: London 1961)

KNIGHTLY EPICS

The Song of Roland (tr. D. D. R. Owen: Woodbridge 1990)
The Poem of the Cid (tr. Rita Hamilton and Janet Perry: London and New York 1984)
Heroes of the French Epic (tr. Michael Newth: Woodbridge and Rochester, NY, 2005)

CHIVALRIC LITERATURE

Legends of Arthur, ed. Richard Barber (Woodbridge and Rochester, NY, 2001)
Peter Dronke, *The Medieval Lyric* (Woodbridge and Rochester, NY, 1996)
Jean Froissart, *Chronicles* (selection tr. Geoffrey Brereton: London and New York 1968)

THE CRUSADES

Steven Runciman, *A History of the Crusades* (Cambridge and New York, 1951)
The Siege of Malta (Woodbridge and Rochester, NY, 2005)
Helen Nicholson, *The Knights Hospitaller* (Woodbridge and Rochester, NY, ...)
William Urban, *The Teutonic Knights* (London and Mechanicsburg, PA, 2003)
Malcolm Barber, *The New Knighthood: A History of the Order of the Temple* (Cambridge and New York 1994)

TOURNAMENTS

Richard Barber and Juliet Barker, *Tournaments: Jousts, Chivalry and Pageants in the Middle Ages* (Woodbridge and New York 1989)

Index